MESSAGE OF THE SACRAMENTS

Monika K. Hellwig, Editor

Volume 3

Blessed and Broken

An Exploration of the Contemporary
Experience of God in Eucharistic Celebration

by

Ralph A. Keifer

 Michael Glazier, Inc.
Wilmington, Delaware

Second printing 1984

First published in 1982 by Michael Glazier, Inc., 1723 Delaware Avenue, Wilmington, Delaware 19806. Distributed outside the USA and Canada by Gill & Macmillan, Ltd., Goldenbridge, Inchicore, Dublin 8.

Library of Congress Catalog Card Number: 82-80193
International Standard Book Number:
    Message of the Sacraments series: 0-89453-226-4, Paper; 0-89453-280-4, Cloth
    BLESSED AND BROKEN:
        0-89453-267-7, Paper; 0-89453-393-2, Cloth (Michael Glazier, Inc.)
        7171-1135-0 (Gill and Macmillan, Ltd.)

Cover design by Lillian Brulc
Printed in the United States of America

CONTENTS

IN MEMORIAM
MARY FRANCIS WILKINSON
who
must have found Jerusalem
for
she prayed much.

Your longing is your prayer;
and if your longing is continual,
then you pray always.

St. Augustine

INTRODUCTION

One of the constant experiences of a theologian is that a vast number of people, even among serious believers, simply can make no sense of any number of items in the traditional repertoire of Christian beliefs. If one listens carefully, it becomes apparent that the major issue is not the truth or falsity of certain teachings, but the problem that they simply seem to make no sense. They have no connection with reality as it is actually experienced. Henri Nouwen notes this in his *Genesee Diary*.

> For the past few weeks we have had a Friday night lecture by a visiting seminary professor. He has been speaking about the doctrine of the Trinity and especially about the Holy Spirit. For me these lectures are a special experience. ... I like the lectures, I am intrigued, I don't want to miss them — but at the same time I feel dissatisfied on a level I did not understand in the past but is now closer to my consciousness. . . I kept saying to myself, "How interesting, how insightful" — and at the same time I said to myself, "So what? What do all these words about God and the Father, the Son, and the Spirit have to do with men here and now?" As soon as I step outside the circle of his terminology, which is very familiar to me, the whole level of discourse seems extremely alienating.[1]

Those who are serious about the meaning of the holy

[1] Henri Nouwen, *Genesee Diary*, (Garden City: Doubleday, 1976), pp. 149,150.

eucharist are no exception. They find themselves untouched by traditional issues such as the real presence of Christ in the eucharist or the sacrificial character of the eucharist. It is not that they question the truth of these things. It is simply that such categories seem not to speak to them any more. My own field of expertise, liturgical studies, has attempted to renew eucharistic understanding by resorting to equally traditional, but largely forgotten categories — thanksgiving or blessing, and memorial. When one moves away from the enthusiasm of the minority who discourse about these things, there is something equally abstract about this new attempt. Other sorts of study have fared no better. Systematic theology has concentrated on eucharist as symbol, and on the category of meal, with similar results — a resounding "So what?" Almost all contemporary commentary on the eucharist leaves one with the impression that it belongs to a world of textbooks, chalk and blackboards, at best to the world of the lecture, and not at all to the world of love and work, struggle and prayer that is the heart of the life of faith.

After lecturing on the eucharist to audiences which have included everyone from seminary professors with doctorates in theology to ordinary lay people with no special theological education, I am not convinced that this painful impasse between theology and life is the fault of the people who are saying "So what?" The impasse cannot be attributed to a loss of faith and it cannot be attributed to intellectual laziness. It belongs, rather, to a profound change of religious consciousness which is now beginning to surface vigorously in American Roman Catholicism. It is a process which is as inexorable as it is profound. People simply experience God in a different way than their ancestors in faith did. And that experience radically shapes their perceptions of who God is and who they are in relation to God. It inevitably shapes their perceptions of sacraments.

As I hope to suggest in this book, that new experience of God is shaped by the circumstances of our own time and is inherent in the church's liberty to live the gospel in such a way as to speak to all times and all situations with its message of freedom and wholeness that we call salvation. What is happening is not a change in faith, but a profound change in the experience of faith, which in turn calls for a change in the formulation of faith.

This new experience of God is the result of the scientific revolution. The scientific revolution is at last coming home to Roman Catholicism in the United States. This does not mean that science is or ought to be the measure of all things and all knowing and all understanding. It certainly does not mean that everybody is a scientist or that everybody is even interested in scientific issues. It simply means that because of certain changes of perception brought by the scientific revolution, we in fact experience the world in a very different way than our ancestors did. I think this is readily illustrated by something we are all familiar with: the insurance companies' description of natural disaster as an "act of God". We all know that the term "act of God" means natural disaster. We also experience the expression as extremely quaint. It has nothing at all to do with the shape of our own believing. That God, for instance, would destroy innocent people's property and damage innocent people's lives with lightning is either absurd or revolting to contemporary religious perception. This is the direct product of the scientific revolution — having come to understand something of meteorology and the workings of static electricity, it is no longer possible to interpret a lightning strike as a divine intervention.

The wider horizon of this changed consciousness is that the world became an infinitely more interesting place when we discovered the microscope for the exploration of the world's inner workings and the telescope to look outward into the universe. Harnessed first to westward expansion and the exploration of the Americas, and now to potential space travel, these inventions have made the world an interesting and exciting sort of place as never before. In the wake of the scientific revolution, another revolution has come, too, the beginnings of the exploration of human space —

inner human space in psychology and related fields, outer human space in anthropology, sociology and related studies. With an ever more sophisticated technology at our disposal, the vistas before us seem endless.

This radically conditions our perception of the world because the world is an ever more human world, a world accessible to us in human terms, a world to be explored and touched. When life was shorter and the world and ourselves seemed simpler, there was more room for God.

But we are beginning to experience the dark underbelly of this new scientific world as well. A generation ago, the technology of a civilized Western nation virtually annihilated the Jewish people from Europe, and brought the whole of Europe into ruins. The precariousness of our world is coming home to Americans now in the tragedies of Vietnam and Watergate, and the ecological crisis which was an abstraction to many a few years ago has become real in the petroleum crisis. Stanley Kubrik's epic films, *2001* and *The Shining*, reflect accurately the world we live in — a world totally pregnant with human possibility, yet darkly shadowed by our own propensity to become tangled in the hells of our own inner space, a world where the machine is both threat and savior.

This is why it has become so difficult to make sense of traditional reflections on the eucharist. It is a fundamental Catholic perception that the eucharist sums up what the whole of faith is about. And so if the eucharist is not seen to connect with that human world we inhabit, in all its glory and all its tragedy, the ready response is indeed, "So what?" It is no longer possible to begin with the traditional categories of sacrifice and real presence because the whole world that revolved around those categories has shifted. The way in which the understanding of those realities was formulated was dependent upon an entirely different view of the world than one in which we now live. We must begin, if we are to begin anywhere, with the two things that are accessible to us — the present experience of eucharistic celebration and our present experience of the world. For if the Incarnation of the Son of God means anything, it means that our only access to God is a human one, and if sacraments mean anything, they mean that the Creator and Giver of life is known through the creatures that are the image of God's glory.

In harmony with the attempt to be responsive to a post-scientific view of the world, I make no attempt to grapple with the doctrines of real presence or eucharistic sacrifice "in themselves", i.e., in terms of what they might mean metaphysically. The burning questions do not lie at this level. Post-scientific people are much more inclined to want to know how something works than why it is or what its metaphysical nature might be, and this is as true of the data of faith as it is of things we can put under a microscope.

What this book attempts, then, is a contemporary theology of the eucharist, attentive not so much to the traditional questions revolving around why and for what purpose, and more to the shape of the experience of the eucharist, which radically conditions how we perceive its meaning. I have purposely written it in a language as accessible as possible to a public larger than the theologically degreed. In attempting a theology of eucharistic experience, one had best be attentive to the experience of ordinary people. The burning religious questions of our time, even when they are posed as "why" questions are actually "how" questions. If we ask, for instance, why a tragedy occurred, it is no longer satisfactory or meaningful for us to attempt to ponder the mystery of God's reasons for permitting it to happen. What we are really asking when we say "why" is "how" — how may I continue to believe, hope, pray in the face of tragedy? The yearning of contemporary faith is not so much to answer the metaphysical questions as to find a way to trace the shape of its own believing. Much theology falls on deaf ears, not because it is false, but because it is inattentive to the shape of people's believing.

To speak of "contemporary experience" is not of course to speak of everyone's experience. In that sense, there is no such thing as "contemporary experience," but only a multiplicity of experiences. What I mean by "contemporary experience" is that which is the experience of significant numbers of people in our time, and which in fact appears as new and unique to our own time. Some people go on experiencing the world and their faith more or less as their ancestors did, even while a new consciousness is emerging.

The sparsity of technical language and notes is in keeping with my wish to continue what has been the most important component of the book — dialogue with people who are not professional theologians. I am concerned to communicate here what has been as much the result of those conversations as it has been the product of research. In fact, the book would not have been written in this form at all if it had not been for the constant discovery of people who find themselves thrown into a new stance of faith, but like St. Paul, blind with the new light, and like old Zachary, dumb for want of words to name what they have found. It is especially because of them and for them that I write.

I owe a special debt of gratitude to my students at St. Mary's Seminary in Baltimore, the Summer Graduate Program of Liturgical Studies at Notre Dame University, and above all, the Catholic Theological Union at Chicago and McCormick Theology Seminary. Reflection with them has been a gift and a privilege. Above all, I must thank Mr. William Freeman who so vigorously challenged me to a new way of doing contemporary theology, and Kathleen Sullivan-Stewart, who encouraged me to write as I have. While I in no way hold her responsible for anything I have written, I am deeply grateful to Dr. Anne Jones for the kind of theological reflection which I was able to take as a starting point. Finally, I wish to thank Father Jan Michael Joncas for the use of his hitherto unpublished poetry, and for valuable reflections along the way.

CHAPTER I

BLESSING AND BREAKING
Contemporary Eucharistic Experience

When I give talks on the sacraments, people regularly ask why the Mass is not better explained to them. I have often been puzzled by the question. All too frequently, I have felt that the celebration of the eucharist is commented unto death, with myriad interventions by priest and commentator. It has finally occurred to me that people really mean that some of their basic experience of the eucharist remains uninterpreted. Part of that experience today includes a certain tension, a sense of disjuncture. My teens tell me that Mass in the parish church is "boring". There are other voices, too, which speak for a yearning for what they call a "sense of mystery" which is felt to be lost from the Mass. We have become a generation of eucharist shoppers, avoiding this one because it is "too long", that one because it lacks a "sense of community". Others, while they experience less of these sorts of tensions, find themselves with a vague sort of uneasiness. They feel a contrast between the way they used to experience the Mass and the way they do now, and wonder vaguely if their faith is slipping. There is a sense of no possibility to return to the past, yet there remains a nostalgia for its clarity, its security, its comfortableness.

These tensions are real, and there is no sign that they are about to go away. If people are less vocal about them than they were a few years ago, that does not mean that the issue has been settled. It simply means that people have learned that complaining about things does not necessarily change them. And it means that a considerable number of people now feel free to stay away quietly. If our present experience of the eucharist is fraught with tension, it is a fact worth serious reflection. That does not necessarily mean that the tension can be resolved. There are no guarantees that belief will be a comfortable thing. In fact, there are any number of sayings of Jesus that point to exactly the opposite. Tension at the heart of the church's prayer is not necessarily a bad thing. The issue is not the tension, but what it means. In fact, how we interpret that tension will have everything to do with whether it is liveable or not. For instance, if I am prone to headaches, I will be considerably more distressed if I assume that I have a brain tumor than if I discover I need to be fitted for eyeglasses. Or if I am at a party and find myself uncomfortably warm, I will be much happier assuming that the room is overheated than I will be if I assume that I am sporting a fever.

And so one of the major purposes of this book is to reflect seriously upon the tension we experience with the eucharist, to strive to make some sense of it in terms of who we are as a people who believe. It is a truism of the spiritual life that difficulty with prayer is not necessarily a sign of regression or disaster. It may in fact signal the onset of a new stage of life and growth. There is no reason why this should not be as true of the church as a people as it is true of individuals.

There is an old liturgical axiom, *lex orandi legem statuat credendi*, the rule of prayer establishes the rule of faith — or less pedantically translated, the way we pray is the way we will believe. This does not have to do simply with prayer texts, the words that are used, but with the very texture of prayer, the way of praying that includes not only words but also gestures, and not only gestures, but gestures which speak for unvoiced attitudes, lived assumptions which are imaged in the act of praying. There is no "mere" style of prayer. Any halfway coherent liturgy flashes out a view of God and the world, of the church, its mission and ministry, of the relationships between believers. It does that in its very "style". It will speak for a particular vision of who Christ is, as it will speak for the way it understands our relationship to him. This is the reason why the simplest changes in the rite of Mass are so readily attended by controversy, and why such apparently insignificant details of ceremonial as receiving communion in the hand or using real bread at the altar, can become the subjects of years-long international debates. Varied usages speak for very different views of the world, of God, of Christ, of the church, of ministry — of, in fact, everything important that faith is about.

If we are to begin to understand our present situation, it will be useful to compare the texture of eucharistic celebration before Vatican II with the texture of our present experience of the Mass. For much of our tension is actually rooted in the sense of disjuncture between those two expressions of the Catholic eucharist. The two different ways of celebrating Mass speak for two very different worlds of religious perception. And naturally, caught between those two worlds, we experience them at war within us. Our architecture of transition, with its unused "high" altar and the new table facing the people, or brand new churches which people describe as "cold", or "empty" speak worlds for a people who stand between the times.

We need to begin, then, by examining the differences between the experience of eucharist half a generation ago and today's experience of it. For our problem, if problem it is, is that we experience a real discontinuity with our recent religious past.

Perhaps the most obvious difference between eucharistic experience now and half a generation ago is that the new rite functions basically as a welcome to the eucharistic table, the old rite was experienced as a sacrificial action. The Baltimore Catechism described the Mass before Vatican II as "the unbloody sacrifice of Calvary," in other words, as a sacrifice in commemoration of the death of Christ for the forgiveness of sins. To describe it in this way was to state what was obvious to the simplest believer — that the action of the eucharist was experienced as an event of petition in atonement for sin. "Deliver us. . . we beseech you. . . have mercy on us sinners. . ." These are the themes endlessly repeated in the old Mass ritual, from the priest's and server's Confiteor at the foot of the altar right through even to the last and latest prayer to St. Michael the Archangel. Often enough, the first audible chanted words of the sung Mass were *Kyrie eleison*, Lord, have mercy; and the last spoken words of low Mass were "Have mercy upon us." Purificatory rituals attended every significant action, from the beginning of Mass through the communion.[1] Some of them were very elaborate — the old offertory rite was basically such a rite of purification, and it was very lengthy and involved. The most frequently used gestures by the laity — kneeling and beating the breast — were themselves penitential. And only a generation ago, most people were uneasy approaching communion without first going to confession.

It is a parody both of the piety of people before Vatican II and of the rite itself to assume that what this spoke for was a kind of craven cringing before a wrathful God. Often enough — and this shone through both the chants and the ritual — the rite spoke tenderly and joyously of a merciful God. But certainly, what was in the forefront was a consciousness of coming before God as sinners. The basic impact of the rite was that it was a dramatic intercession for the sins of the world. This was underscored in the great Canon, the central eucharistic prayer. It was developed as a grand prayer of petition, and the gestures and language of the priest joined with the art and architecture of most churches to make the Latin Mass a truly powerful intercessory event. Speaking of the sacrifice of Christ, the Epistle to the Hebrews sums up the meaning of the sacrifice in the following lines:

> "You stand before mount Zion and the city of the living God, heavenly Jerusalem, before myriads of

[1] For a full account of this development, see J.A. Jungmann, *The Mass of the Roman Rite*, (New York: Benziger, 1950), 2 Vols.

> angels, the full concourse and assembly of the first-born citizens of heaven, and God the judge of all, and the spirits of good men made perfect, and Jesus the mediator of a new Covenant, whose sprinkled blood speaks more graciously than the blood of Abel." (Heb. 12:22 ff)

With the altar high atop a series of steps, dominated by the crucifix and surrounded by the statues of the saints, as the Latin Mass was performed with solemn chant, mysterious murmur, and stately ceremonial, the simplest believers could kneel before the awesome rite and feel themselves present "before Mount Zion".

The use of the Latin language was in many ways no barrier to understanding. The rite spoke for a God who condescends in his mercy to reach out to us sinners. Speaking as the liturgy did for a God who was seen as in some ways distant, and in every way mysterious and awesome, the use of a special language was, if anything, experienced as entirely appropriate.

What gave the rite its dramatic power and awesomeness was not simply its beauty of design. In ritual, beauty of design only appeals to the extent that the design mirrors people's perceptions of their world, their God, and of themselves as a people. Contrary to what some people assert, a liturgy never simply "speaks for itself". Rather, it "speaks" within a particular set of presuppositions — presuppositions not only about what the Mass is about, but also presuppositions as to what the whole life of faith is about. In other words, a liturgy speaks for a people's religious values, and it will remain in vigor as long as those values are vigorously held. It will lose its power once it ceases to be a faithful mirror of people's presuppositions.

Now one of the obvious presuppositions of the old rite of Mass was that a central item in the relationship between ourselves and God is our condition as sinners. That rite simply makes no sense on any other grounds than the presupposition that the basic item in our dealing with the

Almighty is to deal with our own sinfulness. What gave the rite its dramatic power was not simply that it was good sanctuary drama. It was also a faithful image of the way the church of the time understood its own functioning. In the medieval church, where the old rite had its origins, all pastoral care was focused on the care of penitents. The major purpose of preaching, for example, was understood as to bring people to the confessor, and the event of confession was seen as the major instrument of the pastoral care of individuals.

And this had everything to do with the role the church assigned the priest at the altar. In the ordinary, everyday life of the church, *the* important ministry was seen as the ministry that involved the "power of the keys," that is, the ministry that involved hearing confessions and giving absolution. The role of the priest at the altar as mediator between God and ordinary people only reflected the role the priest was seen as having in the daily life of the church.

This in turn had everything to do with the understanding of the church. That understanding of the church included the placing of a high premium on priestly mediation, and with it, a high premium on approaching God through the right channels — what theologians now call an "institutional" model of the church. Those values were amply reflected in the rite of Mass. For example, the preparatory rites (entrance, offertory) were elaborated as preparations of the priest, culminating in the preparation of his holy hands for the offering of sacrifice. Likewise, in its prayer for the church, the Canon put prayer for the hierarchy ahead of prayer for the local assembly (ancient eucharistic prayers of a previous time had never even mentioned the hierarchy). The scrupulous way in which every detail of the rite had to be observed reflects those institutional preoccupations, and so does the very language of its prayers. The center of the Canon was the consecration, and the way it is developed highlights a certain legalism. Just before the consecration, the prayer requests that God will find the sacrifice "benedictam, adscriptam, ratam, rationabilem, acceptabilemque."

This translated literally in old missals as "blessed, approved, right, reasonable, and acceptable", and it comes out in official translation as something lovely but entirely different — "Bless and approve our offering; make it acceptable to you, an offering in spirit and in truth." But the virtually untranslatable real sense of the Latin is: "May this offering be acceptably signed, sealed, and delivered before you." Likewise, the story of the last supper (institution narrative) which follows partakes of that legal spirit. Coming as it does after a petition that the bread and wine will become the body and blood of Christ, the story of the last supper is presented as a kind of warrant, the citing of a legal precedent for the doing of the eucharist. Not unaccountably, many priests stuttered over this part of the prayer, in the effort to say the correct words as correctly as possible.

This kind of understanding of the church, with its prizing of priestly mediation and institutional values, contained within it an implied understanding of Christ as well. The high moment of the old rite of Mass was the consecration, when Christ became present under the forms of bread and wine. Everything led up to that awesome moment, and everything else was subordinated to it. The Canon was constructed as a kind of sonar chalice around a pool of silence — before the consecration, the chant died away, and the priest murmured silently at the altar. Only the soft tinkle of sanctuary bells marked out the awesome moment. Everything was marked out as special for that moment — special gestures, with the priest lifting the host and then the chalice, with elaborate genuflections; special materials for the vessels; special coverings for the altar; even special positions for the priest's fingers. Such an approach to the consecration spoke eloquently for an understanding of Christ as the divine and exalted one mysteriously entering an alien world. Even in its most intimate and powerful image of incarnation, the medieval rite projected a sense of Christ's otherness and distance from ourselves.

That understanding of Christ was coherent with a whole world of religious values. The same period which produced the old rite of Mass also took special delight in concentrating on special details of the life of Jesus — his virgin birth and his miracles. And it exalted the images of those details in the saints who were virgins, ascetics, and wonderworkers. Not unexpectedly, it saw life in a celibate religious community as the ideal way of living the Christian life.

The perhaps unintended result of liturgical reform has been to create the preconditions for an utterly different experience of faith than the old Mass rite addressed. Probably, there were five reforms that were the most significant. The first of these was to separate the liturgy of the word (the service of readings) from the altar. In the old rite, the scriptures were usually read at the altar itself, virtually always by an ordained minister, and virtually never facing the people. Also, adult lay ministers were introduced, the priest was positioned facing the people for the eucharistic prayer, the vernacular language was introduced instead of Latin and four, and then eventually nine, official eucharistic prayers took the place of the old Canon. While these looked like "merely" ceremonial changes, they have proved to have the potential for reflecting a very different experience of faith.

First, the matter of reading the scriptures directly to the people in their own language. The old rite, with its merely ceremonial use of scripture (they were read in Latin) strongly suggested that the dialogue between God and his people is over and done with, that nothing new can happen, and that all that has to be done is to preserve the tradition of the past. This is a point of view that is projected in the Canon — whereas older prayers spoke of the present church as the saints of God, the Canon spoke of God's saints in the past tense. And where prayers once prayed for the continuing work of the Spirit and the coming of the kingdom of God, the Roman Canon prayed for the preservation of the institutional church. The proclaiming of the scriptures in the language of the people, however, suggests that the dialogue between God and his people is ongoing, that each generation must hear the message afresh and in its own way.

So, too, that point of view is reflected in the newer eucharistic prayers: ". . . from age to age you gather a people to yourself," as Eucharistic Prayer III has it.

Add to that deritualization of the scriptures the presence in the sanctuary of adult lay ministers, and the liturgy speaks for a church in which there is not simply one ministry but many, as it suggests that the functions of ministry are shared functions. The ministry of the priest is no longer seen as an exclusive one, and the priest (at least potentially) becomes but one minister among many. This will especially be true if it is in any way known that lay people perform significant ministerial tasks in the parish (e.g., counseling, teaching, or visiting the sick), and all the more so if the ministry of the word is grounded in shared study, prayer and dialogue between clergy and laity.

For the priest to pray in our own language, facing us, radically changes his relationship to the people. It makes him a partner in dialogue with us before God. That position also imaginatively locates God in a very different place, and therefore has the potential for rearranging people's vision not only of who God is, but also of who they are in relation to God, and how God is communicated to them. In the old rite of Mass, the priest was manifestly a mediator between God and the people, one who stood in the breach between an awesome God and a suppliant people. The priest's use of a special language heightened both the sense of the people's distance from God (and from the priest) and their sense of the priest's special channels of communication with God. The use of that special language in a fixed text went a long way toward speaking eloquently for a conception of priestly ministry as possessing power over mediating God to people by knowing and using the correct formulae. All of this is signaled dramatically in the difference between "ideal" church architecture before Vatican II and now. Before Vatican II, the priest ascended a flight of steps and stood with his back to us at a "high" altar. Now, he faces us across a table. The older position speaks for mediation, for acting as a spokesman. The newer speaks for hospitality, engagement, involvement. It is interesting to observe that most of the gestures of the priest are the gestures of hospitality — welcoming, invitation. Having had the opportunity to observe eucharistic celebration from behind the priest, I note that most of the present celebrants' gestures involve a kind of sustained ritual "hugging" of a congregation. It is not surprising that the question of the ordination of women is now being raised. The priest's gestures at the altar are those we associate in our culture more with mothering than with a male role.

In the new rite, on the other hand, God is revealed as the One who is named in the exchange between priest and people, a God whose presence is only best and fully known when all have been heard from. The elaborate ritual dialogue which precedes the Preface ("Pray my brothers and sisters . . . . . . The Lord be with you. . . " etc.) places the celebrant in the position of asking the people's permission to speak to God on their behalf. Prayer (and therefore the naming of God) thus depends as much on the people as it does on the priest. The models of what it means to be a lay person and what it means to be a priest are both radically changed. In the old rite, you "heard Mass" — you were the passive recipient of ministry. In the new, you are invited to active engagement. And where in the old rite, the priest stands forth as the bearer of traditional authority, in the new, the stress falls much more on the priest's role as careful listener and able spokesman for those who gather around the Lord's table. So much is this the case that even within the rather inhibited circumstances of ordinary eucharistic celebration, a congregation will suddenly "come alive" when confronted by a celebrant who is experienced as a good listener.

All of this adds up to a very different valuation of both the church and of ourselves as individuals. The use of the vernacular language, the positioning of the priests, and the introduction of unordained but functional adult ministers serves to radically localize the eucharistic event. The old rite, with its carefully observed rules and strictures, spoken in a foreign language by a representative clearly *not* in dialogue with the people present, reflected a style of faith which centered on an objective tradition handed on from somewhere else in time and space. But as the new rite speaks more and more for the immediacy of dialogue between people and ministers, it speaks less for that kind of objectivity, and more for fidelity to the experience of the community here and now assembled.

All of this, I might hasten to add, is not necessarily what people experience every time they go to Mass. But the kind of experience I describe is projected often enough, at least, that many people can hope for it and look for it. Even those who react negatively are a witness to the power of the new message — they have rightly perceived that the new rite of Mass says certain things which the old did not.

The transformation of values in the new rite of Mass is perhaps best witnessed in the ease with which communion in the hand became popular. Given our heritage, where the relation of clergy to laity has been one of ruler to ruled, the active taking of the eucharistic bread from the priest speaks for an entirely new world of religious perception. It is saying, among other things, "I will take what you have to offer, Father, but on my terms and in my way; and you in turn must live with the risk that I will handle what you have to offer in an appropriate and responsible way." What is at stake is not simply the handling of the eucharistic body of Christ, but the very way in which tradition is mediated within the body of Christ that is the church. The event of communion in the hand speaks for a Christ present within the whole church, clergy and laity, a Christ present in the midst of their common sharing and caring. It speaks too for a laity who now perceive themselves not simply as passive recipients, but the active bearers of a religious heritage.

If the old rite's portrayal of Christ tended toward a portrayal of him as the exalted and divine mysterious Other, the new rite certainly tends to a different image of Christ, a Christ within and among those present around the altar. It is a fact that the new rite of Mass lacks a certain sense of mystery. The old rite focused the coming of Christ in the consecration at the hands of the priest. The new is not so dramatically focused. If the eucharistic prayer has a dramatic peak, it is no longer the consecration but the great elevation at the end, when the priest prays, "... through him, in him and with him ...," and the people respond with the great *Amen*. The common demand to join in these words witnesses the people's new sense of involvement in the eucharistic action. But this gesture clearly speaks, not of an awesome Christ mysteriously now come to be present, but of a Christ who has identified himself with humanity. The very words of the prayer are the priest's and people's assertion of that identification.

The popularity of the preparation prayers over the bread and cup is a witness to that sense of a Christ identified, not so much as One who comes from without, but one who is present within the community, within the natural and ordinary lives of the participants. To speak of bread and wine which are not only the fruit of nature, but also the result of human skill and striving, as potentially the body and blood of Christ, is to speak from a religious perception which makes Christ no stranger to ordinary human life. Interestingly, it is popular piety which demands that these prayers be said aloud — the official Sacramentary only states that they *may* be said aloud, and only when there is no offertory song. This is very different from what happens in actual practice.

That new questions now arise, from the ordination of women and priestly celibacy to the use of real bread at the altar, should be no surprise. In view of the world of values that the new rite of Mass projects, such questions are to be expected. If the priest is perceived more as the nurturing advocate for a community, and less as simply the conveyer of an objective tradition — in other words, if, in terms of the conventions of our own culture, the priest's role is seen as more maternal — it is natural to ask whether women might not be priests. And if Christ is seen as present to our natural lives, as fully identified with humanity, celibacy may well be seen less as an avenue of access to God and more of a possible stumbling block. As for details like the kind of bread used on the altar, or whether or not people should share the chalice, or what kind of material should be used for vessels at the altar — these, too, normally speak for a perception of who Christ is. If he is seen, in the words of Eucharistic Prayer IV, as "a man like us in all things but sin," ceremonial details which stress his otherness are apt to seem out of place.

Finally, it can be noted that all of this adds up to a transformed valuation of ourselves in relation to God. What we are affirming, as we accept the values I have noted here, is that we do not estimate ourselves before God primarily in terms of our view of ourselves as sinners. This does not necessarily involve a denial of human sinfulness. Rather, it means a religious reassessment in which human sinfulness is simply one part of the picture, and sometimes not necessarily the most important part. It means, first of all, a recovery of an estimate of ourselves as creatures, and as creatures who are fundamentally good, and not only fundamentally good, but also made in the image and likeness of God, and therefore called into friendship with him. The God of the old rite is a merciful judge, at best a patient parent. The God of the new is the lover and friend and companion of the human race, perhaps most beautifully portrayed in Eucharistic Prayer IV:

> We acclaim you, holy Lord, glorious in power;
> your mighty works reveal your wisdom and love.
> You formed us in your own image,
> giving the whole world into our care,
> so that, in obedience to you, our Creator,
> we might rule and serve all your creatures.
> When our disobedience took us far from you,
> you did not abandon us to the power of death.
> In your mercy you came to our help
> so that in seeking you we might find you.

Again and again you called us into covenant with you,
as the prophets taught us to hope for salvation.

Father, you loved the world so much that in the
fullness of time you sent your only Son to be our Savior.
Incarnate by the Holy Spirit, born of the Virgin Mary,
he lived as one of us, yet without sin.
To the poor he proclaimed the good news of salvation;
to prisoners, freedom;
to the sorrowful, joy.
To fulfill your purpose
he gave himself up to death;
and, rising from the grave,
destroyed death and made the whole creation new.
And that we might live no longer for ourselves
but for him who died and rose for us,
he sent the Holy Spirit,
his own first gift for those who believe,
to complete his work in the world,
and to bring to fulfillment the sanctification of all.[2]

It is here, however, that we are also perhaps most ill at
ease. We are aware of that shift of religious perception, and
remembering the evocative power of the old liturgy, nostal-
gically wonder if we have lost something. We may wonder,
too, if the sobriety with which the old rite spoke to the dark
side of human existence might not be worth a second look.
Here and there, there are worries about eucharistic doctrine.
When the present Order of Mass was first introduced, the
fear that it represented a denial of the church's teaching on
eucharistic sacrifice was voiced very loudly. A new intro-
ductory chapter had to be added to the General Instruction
which accompanied the rite, carefully explaining that no
departure from traditional teaching was intended. Similar
fears sometimes surface in regard to the questions of the real

[2]The prayer is familiar to Roman Catholics in another translation. I have
selected the translation which appears in the new Episcopal and Lutheran service
books; its language is more inclusive in this translation.

presence of Christ under the forms of bread and wine. Gestures like communion in the hand can be interpreted as implying "disrespect" for that real presence. Or describing the eucharist as primarily praise and thanksgiving, or as a memorial, is interpreted as denying the fact of Christ's real presence under the forms of bread and wine.

What is being confused is the difference between official church teaching and the value the living church may put on it in a given period of history, especially the value that piety may put on it. For instance, it is a dogma of the church that Christ will come again in glory to judge the living and the dead. In the first century, that belief so captured the Christian imagination that most of the New Testament would be unintelligible without it. It was still so important in later centuries that it could find its way into the baptismal creed and into the creed at Mass. It had sufficient hold on medieval piety for it to have a central place in religious art right into the Renaissance. Yet it is scarcely a major item in the average modern Catholic's repertoire of beliefs. Catholics can regularly and seriously pray the Lord's prayer without even a thought of Christ's coming in glory, a possibility that would have positively boggled the minds of the first Christians who used that prayer.

Similarly, the dogma of the Trinity, as central in the repertoire of primary truths as the coming of Christ in glory, has waxed and waned as a central item in piety's repertoire. At one time, it animated the Christian imagination in such a way that there was a felt need to make pictures and statues of the Trinity, a great religious order was named after the Trinity, and the feast of the Trinity became a major feast day. This had a powerful stamp on the liturgy. The Preface of the Holy Trinity came to be used on all Sundays of the year outside the great festal seasons of Christmas and Easter and the penitential season of Lent. Yet there is no longer a felt need to "protect" the dogma of the Trinity, much less celebrate it as the piety of an earlier age did. Only a century ago, John Henry Newman could wax lyrical about the Athanasian Creed, the medieval church's grand summation of the dogma of the Trinity. Yet today that creed is virtually unknown even to educated Catholics. The Catholic tradition is rich and wide and deep enough to allow for variation according to the needs and perceptions of various times and places. If our immediate ancestors in faith thrust eucharistic real presence and eucharistic sacrifice to the forefront of their consciousness, it is not necessarily an imperative for us to do the same.

It is a fact of Christian history that even central dogmas are held in various *ways* in different times and places. The image of Christ, for instance, has always been heavily colored by the circumstances of time and place. Christian art is normally a faithful mirror of Christian prayer and teaching. And so when the church was young and fresh and dispossessed by persecution, Christ was portrayed in art as a beardless young man, as he was called in prayer the child or slave of God. Later, when the church became the official religion of the Mediterranean world, Christ was portrayed as an older and bearded teacher-king, and invoked with regal titles. In medieval Europe, the church was at least nominally the final arbiter of right and wrong in society, and her pastoral mission was seen as the care of sinners. And there, the picture of Christ the Judge dominated cathedral doors, as the Mass was seen as averting that dread judgment. And so, if Christ himself can be perceived in various ways at different times and in different places, there can be nothing unthinkable about varying eucharistic perceptions according to the needs of time and place.

A certain selectivity about beliefs seems inherent in the Christian experience. In a eucharistic context, we may observe that the very heart of the eucharist itself shows that sort of selectivity. For instance, for centuries, both piety and theology strove to make as important as possible the expressions "This is my body...this is my blood"; in theology, ritual, architecture, official prayer, popular piety, in hymnody and art, these words were stressed. At the same time, "Take and eat this all of you," could be so ignored that it was acceptable for lay people to approach the altar once a year, while "Take this and drink all of you," was ignored altogether and still is at many eucharistic celebrations. As I hope to show in this book, that selectivity is directed by the circumstances of the time and is inherent in the church's freedom to live the gospel in such a way as to speak to all times and all situations with its message of freedom and wholeness that we call salvation. That selectivity is demanded by the fact that the circumstances of those various times and situations condition people's experience of God. And in conditioning people's experience of God, they demand, not a change in faith, but change in the formulation of faith.

At a time when a sense of discontinuity with the immediate past is one of the most important factors in the experience of faith, it may be most reassuring to concentrate on the differences of experience over the ages. If Christ is indeed the Lord of history, then it is only to be expected that Christ will be known only through the special conditions of various times and cultures, and only to be expected that the celebration of Christ's presence will take on a variety of forms. In the coming chapters, we will examine more closely the ways in which the eucharist is being shaped, both in practice and understanding, according to new needs and new religious perceptions in our own time. If the new Mass speaks more for dialogue with one another, and less for the mediation of a tradition, more for a Christ present within the community and less for a Christ mediated to us from without, this is not only because of its liturgical design. It is also because it is being shaped by contemporary perception. In the coming chapters, we will examine more of the relationship between the action of the eucharist and contemporary religious perception.

Recommended Reading

Crichton, J.D., "An Historical Sketch of the Roman Liturgy," in Sheppard L. (ed), *True Worship* (Baltimore: Helicon, 1963), 45-82.

Keifer, Ralph A., *To Give Thanks and Praise* (Washington: National Association of Pastoral Musicians, 1980) [Includes the General Instruction on the Order of Mass, along with commentary].

The Story of the Mass, Vol. 54 (May-June 1978) National Bulletin on *Liturgy,* Canadian Catholic Conference. Ottawa, Ontario, Canada.

CHAPTER II

BEFORE AN EMPTY SKY
The Experience of God
Yesterday and Today

Much of our inherited religious language is a language of intervention, a language which suggests that God is One who intervenes from outside the world, as a kind of invader from elsewhere. God's approach to the world is seen as essentially external; the world is something God acts upon. Like the ruler, or the businessman, or the scientist, God looks at situations, judges the evidence, makes decisions, and carries them out. This is perfectly articulated in Genesis 2, where God is portrayed as a master craftsman. The Lord God "formed man" and "planted a garden," and "made to grow every tree," and he "took the man and put him in the garden." God is as surely an outsider to the world as a little girl is outside her dollhouse arranging the pieces.

What this meant in terms of the perceptions of ordinary believers is perhaps best summed up in a text like the Exhortation from the Order for the Visitation of the Sick in the 1662 Book of Common Prayer. While this is an Anglican source, the text is not in any sense peculiarly "Protestant." It is an admirable summary example of the view of the relationship between God and the world held by most orthodox believers from biblical times almost down to the present. It is also an admirable summary of the view of God's action in the world given classic expression in St.

Augustine's *The City of God.* That the text appears in the
Prayer Book simply points out how fundamentally similar
the basic religious perceptions were among both Catholics
and Protestants. Here is that text:

> Dearly beloved, know this, that Almighty God is the
> Lord of life and death, and of all things to them
> pertaining, as youth, strength, health, age, weakness
> and sickness. Wherefore, whatsoever your sickness
> is, know you certainly, that it is God's visitation.
> And for what cause soever this sickness is sent unto
> you; whether it be to try your patience for the exam-
> ple of others, and that your faith may be found in the
> day of the Lord laudable, glorious, and honourable,
> to the increase of glory and endless felicity; or else it
> be sent unto you to correct and amend in you what-
> soever doth offend the eyes of your heavenly Father;
> know you certainly, that if you truly repent you of
> your sins, and bear your sickness patiently, trusting
> in God's mercy, for his dear Son Jesus Christ's sake,
> and render unto him humble thanks for his fatherly
> visitation, submitting yourself wholly unto his will,
> it shall turn to your profit, and help you forward in
> the right way that leadeth unto everlasting life. Take
> therefore in good part the chastisement of the Lord;
> for (as Saint Paul saith in the twelfth Chapter to the
> Hebrews) whom the Lord loveth, he chasteneth, and
> scourgeth every son whom he receiveth. If ye endure
> chastening, God dealeth with you as sons; for what
> son is he whom the father chasteneth not? But if ye
> be without chastisement, whereof all are partakers,
> then are ye bastards, and not sons. Furthermore, we
> have had fathers of our flesh, which corrected us,
> and we gave them reverence: shall we not much
> rather be in subjection unto the Father of spirits,
> and live? For they verily for a few days chastened us
> for their own pleasure; but he for our profit, that we
> might be partakers of his holiness. These words,

good brother, are written in holy Scripture for our comfort and instruction; that we should patiently, and with thanksgiving, bear out our heavenly Father's correction, whensoever by any manner of adversity it shall please his gracious goodness to visit us. And there should be no greater comfort to Christian persons, than to be made like unto Christ, by suffering patiently adversities, troubles, and sicknesses. For he himself went not up to joy, but first he suffered pain; he was crucified. So truly our way to eternal joy is to suffer here with Christ; and our door to enter into eternal life is gladly to die with Christ; that we may rise again from death, and dwell with him in everlasting life. Now, therefore, taking your sickness, which is thus profitable for you, I exhort you, in the Name of God, to remember the profession which you made unto God in your Baptism. And forasmuch as after this life there is an account to be given unto the righteous Judge, by whom all must be judged, without respect of persons, I require you to examine yourself and your estate, both toward God and man, so that accusing and condemning yourself for your own faults, you may find mercy at our heavenly Father's hand for Christ's sake, and not be accused and condemned in that fearful judgement.[1]

In the Prayer Book text, God is an intervener, a manager and a manipulator. God, we are assured, is the wise parent, at whose hand these things come for our own good. And as the action of God is conceived so definitely and purposively, we are in turn called to a vigorous response — to understand the event, to accept a definite interpretation of suffering. We are, above all, called to repent, to respond to God, ultimately, in terms of our guilt. "All the world is a stage" in a peculiar sense within this religious vision — for the world is

[1] It is based on an earlier, pre-Reformation text in the Sarum Manual for pastors.

simply a scenario, a backdrop, almost, where the drama of the relationship between God and people is worked out in terms of a struggle between vice and virtue. If God is separate from the world, so are people: sickness is given meaning either as training in steadfast virtue or as purification for sin: it is given no significance in its own right.

How different this perspective is from a contemporary reflection on evil in the world by Annie Dillard:

> Into this world falls a plane.
> The earth is a mineral speckle planted in trees. The plane snagged its wing on a tree, fluttered in a tiny arc, and struggled down.
> I heard it go. The cat looked up. There was no reason: the plane's engine simply stilled after take-off, and the light plane failed to clear the firs. It fell easily; one wing snagged in the thin woods where cattle browse; the fuel exploded; and Julie Norwich seven years old burnt off her face.
> Little Julie mute in some room at St. Joe's now, drugs dissolving into the sheets. Little Julie with her eyes naked and spherical, baffled. Can you scream without lips? Yes. But do children in pain scream long?
> It is November 19 and no wind, and no hope of heaven, and no wish for heaven, since the meanest of people show more mercy than hounding and terrorist gods.
> The airstrip, a cleared washboard affair on the flat crest of a low hill, is a few long fields distant from my house — up the road and through the woods, or across the sheep pasture and through the woods. A flight instructor told me once that when his students get cocky, when they think they know how to fly a plane, he takes them out here and makes them land on that field. You go over the wires and down, and along the strip and up before the trees, or vice versa, depending on the wind. But the airstrip is

not unsafe. Jesse's engine failed. The FAA will cart
the wreckage away, bit by bit, picking it out of the
tree trunk, and try to discover just why that engine
failed. In the meantime, the emergency siren has
sounded, causing everyone who didn't see the plane
go down to halt — Patty at her weaving, Jonathan
slicing apples, Jan washing her baby's face — to
halt, in pity and terror, wondering which among us
got hit, by what bad accident, and why. The volun-
teer firemen have mustered; the fire trucks have
come — stampeding Shuller's sheep — and gone,
bearing burnt Julie and Jesse her father to the emergency room in town, leaving the rest of us to gossip,
fight grass fires on the airstrip, and pray, or wander
from window to window, fierce.

So she is burnt on her face and neck, Julie Nor-
wich. The one whose teeth are short in a row, Jesse
and Ann's oldest, red-kneed, green-socked, carrying
cats.[2]

Dillard offers no intellectual resolution. The invitation is
not to active understanding, but to contemplation, to a
sense of both horror and wonder. We are called neither to
learn a lesson, nor to obey a command, but only to be still.
We are called simply to be opened to reality in all its fullness.
And if God is to be found in such experience, it is by
indirection. One may "pray" or "gossip" or "fight grass fires
on the airstrip," or simply "wander from window to window, fierce." But the suggestion is that all are equally
appropriate responses, and all, perhaps, equally necessary if
our response is to be adequate to the event. The vision is
certainly religious: we are called to the fundamental questions of good and evil and meaning in the world. But it is not
a moralizing religiosity. We are called to the contemplation
of a divine presence so utterly pervasive in the world that it
cannot be readily separated from it. One has to pray *and*

[2]Annie Dillard, *Holy the Firm* (New York: Bantam Books, 1979), pp. 31-34.

gossip *and* fight grass fires on the airstrip *and* wander from
window to window, fierce, because if God is to be found at
all in such events, it is in midst of them.

We find a similar vision in a poem by Jan Michael Joncas:

Evensong

sitting on a wooden bench
wrapped in wrinkles and old veils
with eyes the color of wind
she watches twilight kiss her hem

tiny with unspoken dream
a faded china doll from some relentless attic
she hears the oak leaves sigh
and fall

before the street lights broke the dust
I thought I saw some sparrow
leap to the suns of her eyes.

At first sight, the vision is utterly "secular." Except for the
name of prayer, evensong, and the ironic comparison with
the Virgin Mary in the line "tiny with unspoken dream," (the
reverse of Mary, great with the promise of the Messiah)
there is no mention of God. Yet we are invited to the same
contemplation of reality in all its horror and all its splendor,
and thus, implicitly, to the contemplation of the God within
the world. Joncas unfolds this for us more directly in the
following poem:

Dover

outbreasting air and ocean
the schoolboy gulls dive
crested and fearless
before the cliffs

plumed by saltspray
they trust a physics

far from their brains
as God from ours

they cry all the black night
a haunted instinctual music
many times repeated:
so old Job spun his praise

In the religious world of Dillard and Joncas, sacred and profane are not readily distinguished from one another, just as God is no awesome invader from without, but a mysterious presence within. The old woman of *Evensong* represents human pettiness and disappointment and failure, yet within her lies the hope of divine presence. Dillard's scenario is nature (in this case, the horror of accident), and Joncas' is history (the frustration of human striving). Yet in both cases there is a sense of the sacred at the heart of things — in Dillard, communicated mostly by indirection, in Joncas, by way of suggestion.

That sort of religious consciousness is not at all uncommon today. The problem is, it is not often identified as a religious consciousness. Conventional religion, and that includes especially conventional patterns of worship, tends to support the older image of God as an invader from without. People are led to assume that if they can no longer imaginatively conceive of God as one who invades the world, that something has gone wrong with their faith. This can be excruciatingly painful for those who, for one reason or another, are unable to distance themselves from conventional religiosity. The distancing may be internal — one thinks of the religious sister who must grapple with this within the context of a religious community; or external — some people can only cope with the issue by withdrawing entirely from the institutional church, at least for a time. In any case, the distancing is necessary. In one way or another, people must find a sense of authenticity, a sense of connection between their perceptions of reality and what others say reality is about.

It is here that we come to the heart of most current tension about liturgical prayer. Most of our inherited liturgical patterns speak vigorously of God as One who comes from outside the world and enters into it. It was in fact the liturgical dramatization of God's entry into the world which gave the old rite of Mass its awesome sense of mystery. This was not true only of the "moment of consecration." Every detail of the old rite was designed to evoke that sense of God's awesome entry. We can see this, for instance, in the development of the Nicene Creed, the profession of faith still used at Sunday Mass. The stresses are on God's otherness and the awesomeness of Christ. Where the Creed spoke of God's entry into the world through the incarnation, all genuflected, and the chant changed from a major to a minor key. The very text of the creed reflects the highlighting of the incarnation as the entry of the awesome God into the world. Compare the texts of two very different creeds, the Nicene, and the present baptismal creed of the Roman church:

Nicene Creed	Baptismal Creed
We believe in one God, the Father, the Almighty, maker of heaven and earth, of all that is seen and unseen.	Do you believe in God, the Father Almighty, creator of heaven and earth? *I do.*
We believe in one Lord, Jesus Christ, the only Son of God, eternally begotten of the Father, God from God, Light from Light, true God from true God, begotten, not made, one in Being with the Father. Through him all things were made.	Do you believe in Jesus Christ, his only Son, our Lord, who was born of the Virgin Mary, was crucified, died and was buried, rose from the dead, and is now seated at the right hand of the Father? *I do.*

For us men and for our
  salvation he came
  down from heaven:
by the power of the
  Holy Spirit
he was born of the Virgin
  Mary, and became man.

For our sake he was crucified under Pontius Pilate;
he suffered, died, and was
  buried.
On the third day he rose
  again in fulfillment of
  the Scriptures;
he ascended into heaven
and is seated at the right
  hand of the Father.
He will come again in glory
  to judge the living and
  the dead,
and his kingdom will have
  no end.

We believe in the Holy
  Spirit, the Lord, the
  giver of life,
who proceeds from the
  Father and the Son.
With the Father and the
  Son he is worshipped
  and glorified.
He has spoken through the
  Prophets.
We believe in one holy
  Catholic and apostolic
  Church.
We look for the resurrec-
  tion of the dead,

Do you believe in the Holy
  Spirit,
the holy Catholic Church,
  the communion of saints,
the forgiveness of sins, the
  resurrection of the body,
and life everlasting?
I do.

and the life of the world
    to come.   Amen

We may note in passing that the Creed at Mass is no longer
sung. Also, the official direction of the liturgical books that
people should bow at the words "and he was made man" is
universally ignored. There is considerable pressure for the
use of the earlier "Apostles" Creed. All of these develop-
ments are symptomatic of a general shift of religious perception which no longer is so gripped by the thought of God
entering the world from without. The great medieval hymn
of thanksgiving, the *Te Deum,* speaks of the incarnation in
these words, "non horruisti virginis uterum," which are best
translated, "You did not find the virgin's womb abhorrent."
The suggestion, of course, is that there might well be something abhorrent about a connection between the divine Son
and the human womb. Certainly it projects a view of the
incarnation as the entry of an awesome God from without,
and highlights the specialness of the virgin birth as over
against any ordinary human birth.

    This view of God as an outsider entering into the world
through the incarnation was dramatically projected in the
medieval rite of Mass. The Preface, culminating in the chant
of the Sanctus, praises God as the awesome holy One,
stressing his distance from ordinary mortals by speaking
with sonorous cadences of a God whose associates are
literally nothing like anything on earth, the majestic chorus
of angles: "The Angels praise your majesty, the Dominions
adore, the Powers tremble before you. The heavens, and all
the hosts of heaven, as well as the blessed Seraphim, rejoice
together in your company." After the threefold holy, holy,
holy, sung in awed tones, the priest lapsed into solemn
silence to whisper his way into the moment of consecration,
so filled with dread in the medieval heart that the priest's
saying the words of consecration was known in the middle
ages as the "periculum," the place of peril.

    The otherness and specialness of that presence of Christ
was protected in every way possible, from language in the

consecration narrative which stressed it ("he took bread into his *holy and noble* hands." The adjectives do not occur in any biblical text), to ceremonial details which emphasized it (an intense scrupulosity about the handling of the bread and the wine, a scrupulosity so intense that both the use of real bread and the laity's communion from the chalice were eventually given up), to practices utterly unthinkable to earlier generations, such as the laity's abstaining from communion out of "reverence," right up to our own times.

As I have already suggested, our eucharistic liturgy no longer projects God as coming from without, especially in its primary gestures, those which speak for the relationship between priest, other ministers, people, and the bread and wine they share. For the presider to speak in dialogue across the table, the suggestion is that God is *within* the assembly, that the eucharistic action is experienced not as a making present of an absent Jesus, but a celebration and revelation of his presence.

As long as the experience of God as an invader from outside prevailed, the eucharistic images which clustered about real presence were "invasive," too. Christ was understood as "coming down" on the altar, as entering from without, and the gestures which highlighted that presence were thrusting gestures, the elevation of the host and chalice above the head of the priest. In the new liturgy, where Christ does not so much "come down" as reveal himself as the One who gives the assembly its coherence and meaning, the gestures are invitational, welcoming. In the present rite of Mass, there are five elevations of the eucharistic bread and cup — at the preparation of the altar and gifts (offertory), at the narrative of the last supper we call the consecration, at the closing doxology (through Him, with Him, in Him) of the eucharistic prayer, at the breaking of the bread, and immediately before the communion. In all cases, both word and gesture point to our involvement with Christ in the eucharistic action.

A new eucharistic piety is already being born. The change in eucharistic hymnody reflects the changed perception of eucharistic presence. The classic eucharistic hymns of the medieval period stressed that sense of Christ as the one who represents the God from without. The *Adoro To Devote* (Humbly We Adore Thee) stresses the distance between the Christ present yet unseen and the natural elements of bread and wine: "Humbly we adore thee, God truly hidden beneath these forms of bread and wine." This contrasts directly with a new communion hymn like John Foley's *One Bread, One Body*, which stresses the unity between the people, the elements, and their Lord:

> One bread, one body,
> one Lord of all,
> one cup of blessing which we bless.
> And we though many throughout the earth,
> are one body in one Lord.

The great eucharistic hymn of Holy Thursday, *Vexilla Regis Prodeunt,* stresses the military perception of God by portraying Christ as a triumphant king, the procession with the host being seen as the march of an army in triumph. How much this contrasts with the maternal image of *Come to the Water,* a hymn that lends itself naturally to post-communion meditation:

> O let all who thirst
> let them come to the water.
> And let all who have nothing,
> let them come to the Lord. . .
> bring the children without might
> easy the load and light,
> come to the Lord.

Or the great hymn of Corpus Christi *Lauda Sion,* describes Christ as "Ducem et pastorem," Christ the Lord leader, Christ the pastor (shepherd). Keeping in mind that a medieval pastor was a man of immense power of command, both civil and ecclesiastical, the image projected of Christ is strongly aggressive. Compare those images with the invitational images of Christ in Jack Miffleton's *I Am the Vine:*

> I am one vine growing;
> Come, make your home in me.
> I am one river flowing
> Gently to the sea.
>
> Ref: Come, make your home in me.
> Come, make your home in me.
>
> I am the one bread rising;
> Come, set your hunger free.
> I am the one cup crying;
> Come and drink from me.
>
> I am the Spirit bringing
> Holy fire and light.
> I am the shepherd singing
> Love songs in the night.

The danger of the "invasive" is that its stress on the power to direct, command, and manipulate gives it a real potential for violence. Doubtless, the rejection of images of power among contemporary Christians stems from the corruption of the military and aggressive images of God, Christ, and the church. An image like "soldiers of Christ" too readily speaks of a strident sectarian militancy and a self-righteous, smug sense of otherness. To speak of church officers as possessing power is repugnant because it has too often suggested that they have the right to use that power arbitrarily. To speak of God in images of power is often perceived as projecting caprice. The notion, for instance, that God will judge too readily suggests a celestial busybody.

It might be argued that the traditional images of power need to be rightly understood — that the soldier image speaks of courage and team spirit, that the image of the priest as possessing spiritual power need not suggest that he use it arbitrarily, that the notion that God is judge need not necessarily involve a projection of God as capricious. Compelling as such arguments may be academically, they are not compelling to the contemporary heart and mind. The trauma of our times is the negative experience of power, the seemingly inexorable and unmanageable power of bureaucracy, the power of the mass media, the power of government. The tragedies of Vietnam and Watergate and the horrendous tangle of the energy crisis are beginning to bring home to Americans a suspicion of manipulative power that stands in the shadow of a far more monstrous manifestation of executive power run amok in the modern world — the Nazi Holocaust. In an age when soldiers commanded by men in power sent children to ovens, and did so according to the laws of a supposedly civilized nation, the images of masculine power are rendered suspect in the extreme.

If the danger of the images of manipulative power is that they may be corrupted to suggest violence, the image of a God already present within the world and the community has its own dangers, too. The corruption of invitational images is sentimentality. This is perhaps the greatest danger of contemporary worship — that it does too readily slide into escapism or sentimentality. In this regard, we may observe that too many of the images in Miffleton's hymn are, like much we do in church, simply romantic. Vines are something we find in flowerpots, shepherds in romantic pictures, and bread rising is found more frequently in television commercials than in real life. A hymn, and therefore liturgical experience, has become escapist when such images begin to prevail.

The contemporary experience of God need not be at all sentimental. It can at times be searing, as in Dillard's reflections or Joncas' poetry. One of the most famous passages in all contemporary religious literature evokes a contemporary experience of God, and it is utterly devoid of any sort of sentimentality. Here is that famous passage from Elie Wiesel's *Night:*

One day, the electric power station at Buna was blown up. The Gestapo, summoned to the spot, suspected sabotage. They found a trail. It eventually led to the Dutch Oberkapo. And there, after a search they found an important stock of arms.

The Oberkapo was arrested immediately. He was tortured for a period of weeks, but in vain. He would not give a single name. He was transferred to Auschwitz. We never heard of him again.

But his little servant had been left behind in the camp in prison. Also put to torture, he too would not speak. Then the SS sentenced him to death, with two other prisoners who had been discovered with arms.

One day when we came back from work, we saw three gallows rearing up in the assembly place, three black crows. Roll call. SS all round us, machine guns trained: the traditional ceremony. Three victims in chains—and one of them, the little servant, the sad-eyed angel.

The SS seemed more preoccupied, more disturbed than usual. To hang a young boy in front of thousands of spectators was no light matter. The head of the camp read the verdict. All eyes were on the child. He was lividly pale, almost calm, biting his lips. The gallows threw its shadow over him.

This time the Lagerkapo refused to act as executioner. Three SS replaced him.

The three victims mounted together onto the chairs.

The three necks were placed at the same moment within the nooses.

"Long live liberty!" cried the two adults.

But the child was silent.

"Where is God? Where is He?" someone behind me asked.

At a sign from the head of the camp, the three chairs tipped over.

Total silence throughout the camp. On the horizon, the sun was settling.

"Bare your heads!" yelled the head of the camp. His voice was raucous. We were weeping.

"Cover your heads!"

Then the march past began. The two adults were no longer alive. Their tongues hung swollen, blue-tinged. But the third rope was still moving; being so light, the child was still alive. . . .

For more than half an hour he stayed there, struggling between life and death, dying in slow agony under our eyes. And we had to look him full in the face. He was still alive when I passed in front of him. His tongue was still red, his eyes not yet glazed.

Behind me, I heard the same man asking:

"Where is God now?"

And I heard a voice within me answer him:

"Where is He? Here He is—He is hanging here on this gallows. . ."

That night the soup tasted of corpses.[3]

That this is material for prayer can be seen in the following passage from the same author:

At the appropriate moments Gregor recited the Kaddish, that solemn affirmation, filled with grandeur and serenity, by which man returns God his crown and his scepter. He recited it slowly, concentrating on every sentence, every word, every syllable of praise. His voice trembled, timid, like that of the orphan suddenly made aware of the relationship between death and eternity, between eternity and the word.

He prayed for the soul of his father and also for that of God. He prayed for the soul of his childhood and, above all, for the soul of his old comrade, Leib the Lion, who, during his life, had incarnated what

[3]Elie Wiesel, *Night*, (New York: Avon Books, 1969), pp. 75, 76.

is immortal in man. The last Kaddish would be for him, to ask that the warrior find peace; that the angels, jealous of his strength and, above all, of his purity, cease to persecute him, that he himself cease to cause suffering to those who once loved him and still love him. Yes, the last Kaddish would be for him, our messenger to heaven.[4]

If eucharistic prayer is to tap into this sort of honesty and wholeness, we need to examine both our situation and our roots more carefully. Never before in the history of the church has there been such constant criticism of patterns of worship as there has been in our own time. Much of that criticism is right and appropriate, however mistaken some expressions of it may be. There are a variety of ways in which contemporary eucharistic celebration can be profoundly alienating, cutting us off both from an authentic experience of God and an authentic vision of the world. Certainly worship is alienating if it still suggests that God is best conceived as "out there," apart from our world. The possibility of the existence of such a God is not merely meaningless to contemporary experience. It is positively revolting in the face of events like the Holocaust, as it is revolting in the face of individual tragedies such as the birth of deformed children. We doubtless need to be weaned from the supposed "sense of mystery" which attended the old rites. Much of that "sense of mystery" was sustained at the expense of human dignity. For instance, it could only be sustained at the expense of making the laity the passive subjects of the clergy's ministrations, as it could only be sustained by positioning a rigid separation between sacred and profane, with the suggestion that ordinary people in their ordinary lives belonged to the realm of the profane. We need a new "sense of mystery" now, a sense of a God present to both the splendor and tragedy of human existence.

More recent models of eucharistic celebration — and by

[4]Elie Wiesel, *The Gates of the Forest*, (New York: Holt, Rinehart, and Winston, 1966), p. 226.

more recent I mean those which developed between the fourth and the thirteenth century, and which represent our inherited pattern until Vatican II — did not only speak for an experience of God as one who came from without to intervene in the world. They also spoke for a very different relationship between the church and the world. They were developed to speak for a situation in which the church was truly the "mother and teacher" of the world, a situation in which the church was the dominant force for good in the world. That situation no longer exists. The church since Vatican II sees itself in dialogue with the world, and it sees that world as fraught with potential for both life and death, as the church, too, is no longer conceived as the kingdom of God on earth, but both "holy and always in need of repentance."

If we are to look for useful historic models, then, we must look behind the eucharist of the Christendom of the fourth to the thirteenth centuries. It is to the New Testament and to the age of beginnings that we must turn. This will become all the more evident in the next chapter, where we will explore the interpretation of death and evil which pervaded the inherited liturgy.

Recommended Reading

Leclerc, Eloi, *People of God in the Night* (Chicago: Franciscan Herald Press, 1979).

Schaffer, Ulrich, *Searching for You* (New York: Harper and Row, 1978).

Shea, John, *Stories of God* (Chicago: Thomas More Press, 1978).

CHAPTER III

FROM ONE ALTAR
TO MANY TABLES

The Problem of Sacrifice and the End of the Medieval Roman Liturgy

Catholic worship has become peculiarly self-conscious since Vatican II. Despite an ancient heritage of ritual, and the careful refurbishing of that ritual in the new liturgical book, liturgies must be planned almost *ad nauseam*. Busyness surrounds our events of worship and frustration attends them. There is a frenetic new preoccupation with liturgy, with all its conferences and programs and directors of worship. Yet our time has produced nothing like Merton's *Seasons of Celebration* or Rahner's *The Eternal Year*, spiritual classics which reflected a situation when the liturgy could be experienced as nourishing and sustaining faith. The liturgy seems to be increasingly more work and less worship. Upon close observation, it can seriously be asked whether we still in fact have anything that is truly common liturgy. We have in fact diverse ways of worshipping, and diverse ways of understanding worship, cloaked by common use of liturgical books. As often as not, the texts of the liturgical books are as much prayed *against* as actually constituting the framework of prayer. One thinks, for instance, of the peculiar juxtapositions of sound and spoken prayer that we have come to accept as a matter of course. A sober penitential entrance is bathed with the syrup of a popular sentimental hymn. The classic Canon (Eucharistic Prayer I) is acclaimed with hully gully holy holies. And while communion begins with a sober affirmation of human sinfulness, musicians make of it a moment of exuberant procession. We might well ask what sort of decadence has made us so uncomfortably self-conscious and so strangely confused over our liturgical heritage. Conservatives have blamed the perpetrators of liturgical reform, while we perpetrators in turn tend to blame lack of education and conservatives who will not accept our educating.

In either case, we liturgists are accorded much more power over the liturgy than we actually have or should have. What is actually happening represents a profound spiritual crisis, involving not so much a loss of faith as it does a change in the way many people believe. A faith is lived through the medium of what may be called primary metaphors — primary ways of shaping and expressing faith. Such metaphors shape not only the way people think about their faith, but also the ways they imagine, feel and act it out. In Judaism, for example, God's making a covenant with his people has been such a primary metaphor: to be a faithful Jew is to live out the implications of that covenant. In a religious culture, a primary metaphor appears over and over again in varying configurations. It can be used over and over again because it is found adequate to express a praying people's experience. Primary metaphors are particularly operative in an authentic living liturgy. The metaphor of God's covenant people, for instance, functions this way in Jewish liturgy — to be God's people is found worth praying, singing, dancing, meditating, circumcising, making festival, lamenting about. In the liturgies of the orthodox Christian

East, the breaking in of the kingdom of God functions as such a primary metaphor. It accounts for the worship of Mary as the God-bearer, for the cultivation of the sense of the exotically mysterious, for its joy, for its lavishness, and for the exaltation of Christ's divinity. While primary metaphors find liturgical expression, they have a cultural impact, as also they are rooted in culture. As the metaphor of the covenanted people of God assured Judaism's survival in the face of dispersion and persecution, so also the metaphor of the kingdom of God come upon earth sustained the ethos of the Byzantine empire and the world of Russian czars.

In the Christian West, the primary metaphor for believing gradually became Christ's atonement for sin on Calvary. It is as evident in the design of the cathedral of Chartres as it is in a Bible-belt Jesus Saves sign.

There are many possible understandings of the terms "sacrifice" and "atonement," but in the Christian West they came to mean that Christ's death on the cross paid back to God a debt of injustice incurred by Adam — that the human race owed God perfect obedience, and Jesus made up for Adam's failure. This understanding of original sin and redemption stands at the heart of the paschal proclamation, the Easter Exultet, which is the medieval church's proclamation of the Easter gospel: "Our Lord Jesus Christ paid for us to his eternal Father the debt of Adam, and by his merciful blood cancelled the guilt incurred by original sin." This was of critical importance in medieval Christianity's response to evil in the world. Sin and sickness, death and deprivation were seen as the result of original sin, and between them and chaos stood the cross of Christ. And the eucharist was seen as making present that sacrifice which redeemed the world, the offering of the self-gift of Christ before the Father here and now at this altar. By the thirteenth century, the atonement metaphor had come to dominate the rite of Mass, a place that neither the reformers of the sixteenth century nor the critics of the twentieth have been able to obliterate. In the eucharistic prayer, it is the words over the bread and the cup about Christ's death for the forgiveness of sins that are ritually highlighted — as, significantly, both the Mass rite as a whole and the communion rite begin with expressions of penitence. That rather successful contemporary version of the Roman Canon, Eucharistic Prayer III, carefully articulates the whole point of the Mass in dramatic language, "See the Victim whose death has reconciled us to you." The prominence of the crucifix in our churches and at our altars is but an emblem of what is expressed ritually. And until half a generation ago, virtually all Catholic piety hinged around that metaphor of Christ's atonement for sin, either by way of crucifixion pieties of one sort or another, or through Marian piety invoking the intercession of the sinless one. Significantly, even the most common Catholic rite of blessing, the sprinkling with holy water, is itself a rite of purification.

This shaping of faith around the primary metaphor of Christ's atoning sacrifice was part of what may be described as a whole "ecology" of faith — a religious world of language and perception which articulated the whole of the life of faith in somewhat legal terms. Salvation tended to be seen as a restoration to a pristine state — getting us "back" to the condition of Adam and Eve before the fall, just as the original sin was seen as a sin of lawbreaking, a sin of disobedience. Thus the work of Christ in the world was seen as that of living the perfectly obedient human life, making up for human disobedience, while providing us a way to the obedient life, both by way of example and through the grace merited by his passion and death.

This peculiar formulation of faith has had profound cultural effects. It has on the one hand created something of a sin-obsessed understanding of religion in the Christian West, as also it has promoted an extremely individualistic and private understanding of the life of faith. But on the other hand, the predominance of such a metaphor permitted the release of immense cultural creativity. Since the church was conceived primarily as an agency dealing with human guilt, Western secularity was able to develop and flourish. Politics, the arts, science, and technology, were able to free themselves from the obscurantism of an old and powerful church. And, on the other hand, the church enjoyed a certain autonomy from the vicissitudes of the state and other cultural forces. This has been a situation which has proved particularly creative in the United States, for both church and the wider culture.

There are a variety of symptoms, however, to suggest that Christ's atoning sacrifice on Calvary is ceasing to be a significant primary metaphor for people. The devotional patterns of the past have declined or disappeared, often dramatically. And this has happened not only with "pamphlet" devotions, but also to such central items as frequent confession and prayer for the dead. One can now attend a Catholic funeral and never hear a word about purgatory. In fact, one has to listen very closely to ascertain anything that can properly be described as prayer for the dead. Even our descriptive language has changed — we go to memorial Masses now, not Masses for the dead. Or, to go to the very heart of things, there is a real nervousness about applying traditional sacrificial language to the eucharist. There is also the strange fact that while we use a rite of Mass whose formal words and basic gestures are almost exorcistic, we are inclined to dress it up and talk about it in festal language. The Roman rite of Mass is essentially a very sober rite of impetration for the forgiveness of sins. That is to say, its key words strongly suggest that the whole point of the Mass is to pray for salvation understood as the forgiveness of sin. Yet these are not actually the words that people tend to hear. Nothing of our use of color, or the movement of ministers, or the contemporary gestures of congregations, or the kinds of songs that we sing suggest anything of the kind. And the same is true of other expressions of piety. Some of the most vigorous patterns of contemporary piety are to be found in the charismatic renewal. But here, too, there has been a significant change from the pieties of the past. The nineteenth century revivalism in which pentecostalism has its roots was strongly salvationist — the image of Christ's atonement on Calvary was as central as it was to the Catholic piety of the same period. But the Jesus of new charismatic hymns is not so much Jesus the savior as Jesus Lord, lover, friend, healer. And forming a religious counter-part to the general mania for self-help, the charismatic testimony has far more to say about being healed from one's hangups than it does about being saved from sin and degradation.

Beyond all these symptoms, however, we may note that a more profound change is occurring. The whole "ecology" of faith is changing. Salvation tends to be seen more in terms of coming to full human wholeness, as original sin is seen less as an act than as a condition which militates against that wholeness. Thus the work of Christ in the world is seen in wider terms than simple obedience; it is his *identification* with humanity which grips the contemporary imagination.

How much liturgical change actually had to do with disturbing people's perceptions of what Christian faith is about, is a question not easily answered. Churchmen often underestimate the number of things people will dutifully accept as the price of participation in the church, long after such things have ceased to have any real or compelling meaning. That liturgical change was accepted as readily as it was and that it was followed immediately by the dropping of so many old pieties suggests strongly that by the eve of Vatican II most of the vigor had already gone out of the old pieties. It looks as if people may well have prayed as they did not because they found the old pieties very meaningful, but because they thought they had to pray that way. It is in fact quite probable that if there had been no liturgical change, our churches would be emptier than they are now. Whatever the inadequacies of our new rites, they at least speak for a concern on the part of the church to meet new needs.

At any rate, the causes of the liturgical impasse are not themselves liturgical. A metaphor succeeds or fails in a liturgy because it speaks to and from life; it speaks for one's whole world and its religious perceptions. The liturgy with its strong atonement metaphor fails to work because that metaphor fails to express adequately the religious intuitions of vast numbers of people. In such a situation that metaphor has become dysfunctional.

It must be noted that the dysfunctionality of a primary metaphor has nothing to do with its truth or falsity, but with its usefulness for interpreting reality. Various metaphors coexist with one another and sometimes change place in the course of history, according to their relative importance. We can see this, for instance, in terms of other metaphors, in the shifting importance of Christmas and Easter. When Christians saw themselves as the vanguard of God's work in an alien world, Easter, a celebration of the event of the resurrection, was the most popular festival. When they saw the church more and more as the stable and established mediator between God and the world, Christmas, a celebration more of the doctrine of the divinity of Christ than of the event of the nativity, became the central feast. And as Christianity began to lose its hold on culture, and become more and more a private matter, and often a privatized matter as well, the birth of the Christ child, with a stress on nothing but domestic metaphors, came into vogue. In other words, that God became incarnate in Christ, that Christ rose from the dead, that he was born in Bethlehem, are all equally true. But their import to piety and the life of the church will vary from age to age. One of the most obvious reasons is that many of us are no longer prepared to express our faith primarily in terms of atonement, as we no longer see our relationship to God primarily in terms of our being sinners.

This shaping of faith around the primary metaphor of Christ's atoning sacrifice was part of what may be described as a whole "ecology" of faith — a religious world of language and perception which articulated the whole of the life of faith in somewhat legal terms. Salvation tended to be seen as restoration to a pristine state — getting us "back" to the condition of Adam and Eve before the fall, just as the original sin was seen as a sin of lawbreaking, a sin of disobedience. Thus the work of Christ in the world was seen as on the one hand to live the perfectly obedient human life, and "make up" for human disobedience, while on the other it was to provide us a way to the obedient life, both by his example and by his grace.

Most healthy people in our world are simply not prepared to see guilt as the primary ground of their meeting with God. The rite of Mass commonly begins with the invitation, "In order to prepare ourselves to celebrate the sacred mysteries, let us call to mind our sins." If people had unlearned the habit of treating English spoken in church as if it were Latin (i.e., not to be taken too seriously as meaning anything), plenty of congregations could roar back to that invitation, "But *why?*" Why not, "In order to prepare ourselves to celebrate the sacred mysteries, let us call to mind how much we love one another"? Or, why not, "In order to prepare to celebrate the sacred mysteries, let us think about how good God is"? The beginning of all significant acts of worship with penitential acts strongly suggests that God is only exalted at the expense of human debasement — a suggestion many people are not prepared to take seriously. And in such a context, a Jesus who is primarily a forgiver of sins can be more of an insult than good news. This is not to suggest that what is wrong with the liturgy is references to human sinfulness. It is simply to suggest that people no longer experience the description of ourselves as "us sinners" as adequate to describing what we intuitively sense as our relationship to God. If salvation is seen as wholeness, then prayer must speak for the whole of our lives and not simply for our sense of sinfulness. Much of what repels people as "churchiness" is that the religious is narrowly confined to the moralizingly religious.

So many of the words of the liturgy appear, if one is attentive to them, as exceedingly harsh toward the individual. To begin both the Mass as a whole and the act of communion with expressions of guilt ("I confess...Lord, have mercy...Lord, I am not worthy...") suggests that guilt is the very ground and horizon of our relationship with God. But this is not the only difficulty. In certain significant ways, the problem of evil in the world engulfs the contemporary mind more horribly than it did our medieval ancestors. They only had to deal with Viking invasions and the black death. We are a generation that has witnessed the Holocaust, as with the increase of scientific knowledge, we are aware how true it is that nature is "red in tooth and claw" and we have a sense of the cold immensity of lifeless, dead outer space. All that terrible knowledge renders the Western formulation of original sin suspect, not so much because of what it says about human evil, but because it so neatly absolves God of any responsibility in the whole matter. Neat distinctions about a God who permits but does not will evil become chilling academic games in the face of events like the Holocaust. John Shea speaks for many in his Prayer of Anger:

> ...on the final day of fire
> after you have stripped me
> (if there is breath left)
> I will subpoena you to the stand
> in the court of human pain.[1]

A Christ who atones only for the sin of the human race does not speak to this kind of prayer. Our liturgy needs a stronger echo of Christ's cry from the cross.

For considerable numbers of people, of course, the old metaphors retain their full vigor. It is perhaps one of the reasons why the ranks of fundamentalist churches and fundamentalist movements are swelling. The loss of a primary metaphor will be felt as a loss of faith, and there are some for whom a journey without familiar images is too terrifying. We are always in danger of confusing faith with the images of faith, especially those that are hallowed by time and use.

---

[1]John Shea, *The Hour of the Unexpected,* (Niles, Ill: Argus, 1977) p. 34.

Fundamentalism is not taken seriously as long as it is seen merely as an attitude toward the interpretation of scripture. Its real power lies in its ability to ignite the Christian imagination — and to ignite it precisely with the metaphors that have stood at the center of traditional Western Christianity. Fundamentalism's stand is seen from within as a stand for the traditional faith. And one might add that it is a stand for the traditional articulation of faith.

There is, then, an inevitably broken character to liturgical celebration today — and for the foreseeable future. No adequate metaphor or metaphors have arisen to take the place of the metaphor of atonement sacrifice. What will embrace a more optimistic and holistic religious view of ourselves as individuals, while at the same time taking seriously the evil of the world and in our own hearts? What will speak both for the gracious God by whom we find ourselves so mysteriously haunted, and for seeming dark cold indifference of the universe? Surely bread and wine, those sturdy symbols of both substance and abundance, joined with words about hope and death, taken in festal assembly, yet in starvation sips and fragments, bear within themselves the power to bring forth new metaphors for a new day. So, too, there is a certain rightness in the peculiar juxtapositions of ancient texts in bald new translation with raw young hymns and awkward new gestures. Surely this speaks in its own stammering way for a space where the wisdom of antiquity can join with the freshness of youth to the praise of God.

In any case, a liturgy that stammers may be exactly the appropriate liturgy for our times, as stammering has been the biblical response to God when the divine is met in all its awefulness. Often enough, the language of our liturgy about death and sacrifice seems as out of joint with our style of worship as crucifixes seem out of place amid butterfly banners and flowered vestments. Yet we abandon the death symbolism in the eucharist at our peril. If the eucharist is the summation of Catholic faith, and if Catholic faith has a relation to real life in the world, then the eucharist must address the mystery of death, and evil.

The language of sacrifice has itself become a problem, more radically even than it was a problem for our ancestors. In our culture, the word "sacrifice" means to "to give up," with darker connotations of meaning "to kill." Significantly, the one sacrificial word that has imaginative power in our culture speaks of an unspeakable killing — I refer to the word *holocaust.* It is all well and good for theologians to insist that sacrifice does not "really" mean "to kill." Biblical commentators, for instance, made it clear that the biblical language of sacrifice speaks for life shared, not for killing. But we cannot ignore the obvious fact that all sacrificial language is rooted in the event of slaughter of animals. And the difference between the ancient world's perception of slaughter and our own is that slaughter has itself ceased to be a social event, normally associated with festivity and speaking for shared bonds of family and friendship. Even a generation or two ago, rural people could find positive appreciation of sacrificial language, for the event of slaughter was part of their lives, and it was a social and festival event. Neighbors gathered to help one another, and the implements of slaughter spoke as much for mutual care as for death. With the application of methods of mass production to food production, the event of slaughter has been reduced to a simple killing of an animal. As a result, the language of blood and sacrifice no longer speaks in the same way with the same positive overtones to contemporary people.

The dislocation of language is more severe than we imagine, for it speaks for other dislocations as well. Modern technology has profoundly disturbed the relationship between human beings and nature, a relationship which is as old as the race and yet is inevitably disappearing. In times past, there was a real communion between people and animals which established a link between ourselves and nature. That communion was quite unlike the sentimental "friendship between people today and their pets." It was a communion in a paradoxical interdependence. People were dependent for survival on the very animals over whom they held the power of life and death. And the relationship is properly described as a "communion" — one does not herd cattle or sheep or work with a horse without that mutual attunement between human being and animal. The film *The Deer Hunter* speaks of the sense of terrible alienation which has been induced by technology, and, significantly enough, chooses the dying symbol of the emotive dependency between man and deer to speak for that alienation.

Yet the dark side of sacrificial language as people now hear it may itself be redemptive. If it speaks for a world separated from nature and shadowed by death, then most assuredly it speaks for the world as it is. We doubtless make comfort and coherence too much the standard of "effective" (often meaning simply "pleasing") liturgy. The contemporary experience of God arises in diverse and fragmentary ways. A liturgy which reflects diverse, even cacophonous elements and which includes many fragmentary statements speaks for just that sort of experience. Discontinuity is the hallmark of contemporary experience. We do not live where we work, we inhabit not one community but many groups, we are deeply aware of separation from our past and of differences from one another. *You Can't Go Home Any More* is not simply the name of a novel; it is increasingly the name of all human experience. Too frequently, we strive to make the liturgy coherent, either by removing archaic statements and attempting to contemporize it, or by removing contemporary statements and attempting to make it archaic. Neither approach is adequate, for we do not live in a unified world.

We need to reflect more deeply that one of the first major Christian liturgical efforts, the compiling of what we have come to call the New Testament, involved the juxtaposing of diverse statements of faith — the four gospels and the epistles of St. Paul. Accustomed as we are to hearing these placed side by side, we fail to reflect that they represent not two or three but *five* major (and diverse) interpretations of Christian faith. Some of the passion for coherence (e.g. a totally "contemporary") liturgy arises out of a failure to reflect seriously enough that our deepest need is to grapple with discontinuity, to acknowledge our tension with it, and to work creatively with the materials we have. We tend to revert to a very passive model of listening when it comes to liturgical or biblical text. We assume that the point of using a text is to call us to accept exactly what it says. And so people waste time patching up prayers or "correcting" biblical texts so that they do not say offensive things about wives obeying their husbands or about brethren when they are speaking of the whole community. To be sure, many of our translations could be improved. But our traditional texts still grate on the contemporary consciousness, and even in more faithful translation they would grate. However you cut it, St. Paul thought wives should be submissive to their husbands. But only on a totally passive model of listening need we be troubled by reading this in church. If the event of hearing the good news is an event in which we are actively involved, then we are called upon to struggle with the text. The good news has always been proclaimed within the language and perspectives of particular times and particular places, ever since it was first proclaimed with a Jewish accent. The raw biblical text is not immediately a word of the Lord to us, and the raw prayer in the official book is certainly not our prayer in any literal sense. The biblical text is, first of all, a word to people somewhere else and inhabiting another time than our own. Likewise, the formal prayers are other people's prayers. We use them to put ourselves in dialogue with a tradition wider and deeper than the confines of our own time and space. The point of that dialogue is not to assume the exact stance of our ancestors in faith, but in hearing them and using their words, to shine new and other light on the present. And so the dialogue with the message, the grappling with the tension it brings, is inherent in authentic hearing. We need to observe more carefully that even the most authoritarian of gospels, that according to John, portrays the real disciples of Jesus as those who were willing not only to question him, but those who were willing to question him constantly. If we are to experience God as really speaking, then we must experience ourselves as real hearers, which is to struggle with the message, not act as passively as recorders.

Also, the experience of discontinuity is matched by another contemporary experience — the refusal of separation from the community which bears the tradition. This is especially true of contemporary Catholics. Dissent has emerged as a fact of Catholic life. It is no longer expected that people will meekly accept everything that is said from the pulpit, and people no longer feel compelled to leave the church simply because they disagree with this or that teaching or practice. Authority has had to deal with a high level of dissent, as those who are not in authority are willing to stay with a church where they often disagree with its positions. An authentic liturgical statement, then, will speak for the reality of the situation — that an active dialogue is indeed in progress between the voices speaking for tradition and the voices speaking for new life and new directions. That this dialogue is not always harmonious or painless and that people do not always listen does not make it any the less a dialogue. Real human conversations are normally filled with this sort of hurly-burly, especially those that take place in real live families.

At the heart of liturgical prayer is what is technically called *anamnesis* and *epiclesis,* remembering and invocation. The event of remembering is not simply a passive thinking about the past, any more than the event of invocation is the resigned petition of those who intend to do nothing about the future. To remember in the active sense means just that, to re-member, to grasp our heritage with both hands and grapple with relating it to the present. To remember Jesus is not to think about the past events of the cross and resurrection, but to uncover their lifegiving power within the present moment. To invoke the Spirit is not so much to ask God to do something for us as to commit ourselves to what God intends for ourselves and the world, to enter into the presence of God in the world more fully and more deeply. An authentic liturgy must speak to this authentically, which means that it owns all the brokenness and discontinuity with which we find God present in our world.

Significantly, the new communion rite finds its dramatic finale in the Breaking of the Bread (which would be more obvious if we used real bread). The very invitation is to find a banquet in the fragmentary and fleeting experience of a taste of bread and a sip of wine. The early church, the gospel of St. Luke tells us, knew the risen Lord in this breaking of the bread (cf. Luke 24:13 ff.). We fail to note that in a real sense, he means that we "only" find the risen Lord in the sadness of a journey away from defeated Jerusalem, and "only" in fleeting moments of festivity amid a workaday world, in other words, "only" in the ordinary world we live in. The message of the cross that transcends the cracking of metaphors and traditions is that God is to be found as surely within the terrible gaps of our lives as in the joy of friendship and festivity. The discord and cacophony present in today's worship speaks for its authenticity, not for its decay. In the lostness and longing that this brings forth, we may rightly find our prayer for the coming of the Lord, for in that we own that there we have no lasting city, but seek that which is to come. The experience of liturgical discontinuity and disharmony represents a call to the death of self which is the heart of eucharistic sacrifice.

The issue is not one of discarding the traditional understanding of the eucharist as a sacrifice, but of plumbing the depths of the meaning of sacrifice. One of the obstacles which sometimes inhibits our entering that spiritual and intellectual struggle in a creative way is the assumption that official eucharistic doctrine stands in the way of a renewed understanding of the eucharist. Often enough, doctrine is perceived as a mental and spiritual straitjacket inhibiting searching inquiry and spiritual struggle. We are prevented from learning from tradition because we assume that tradition is the problem. As I have already suggested in this chapter, traditional *piety* may indeed be part of the problem. But this is not the same thing as traditional *doctrine*.

Doctrine has an important function in relation to piety, sometimes correcting, sometimes affirming it. But in both correcting and affirming piety, it stands in critical relation to it: it does not simply identify the pious inclinations of a particular time or place as *the* teaching of the church.

This critical function of doctrine can be seen in the development of official teaching on the nature of the eucharist as a sacrifice, as well as its teaching on transubstantiation, the technical name of the change by which Christ becomes present under the forms of bread and wine. While the eucharist has been described as a sacrifice from the earliest times, only at the Council of Trent at the time of the sixteenth century Reformation did the Catholic Church formally and solemnly declare itself on the subject of eucharistic sacrifice in official dogmatic teaching. The Council indeed stated in the strongest language that the Mass is a "propitiatory sacrifice," the sacrifice of the cross present in a bloodless manner. But this assertion has to be understood over against what the fathers at the Council of Trent understood to be Protestant teaching. The description of the Mass as a "propitiatory sacrifice" is set over against a view of the Mass as "only a sacrifice of praise and thanksgiving" or a "bare commemoration." That is to say, the fathers of Trent understood certain reformers to be saying that the eucharist is a sacrifice only insofar as it is a thanksgiving for what God has done in Christ in the past, or that it is a commemoration only in the sense of a psychological remembering of Christ's past sacrifice.[2] The concern of the council fathers was to assert that when the eucharist is celebrated, Christ's sacrifice is present in its saving power. In this way, official teaching performed a double critical role: it served to defend the practices of piety (e.g. the desire for Masses for the dead), while correcting views incompatible with traditional under-

[2]For thorough treatment of these issues, see Part III, "The Eucharist as Sacrifice", in *Lutherans and Catholics in Dialogue* I-III, ed. Paul C. Empie and T. Austin Murphy, (Minneapolis: Augsburg Press, 1965); also Anglican/Roman Catholic International Commission, "Agreed Statement on Eucharistic Doctrine," *Worship* 46 (1972) 2-5; *One in Christ* 8 (1972) 69-73; *Catholic Mind* 70 (April 1972) 57-61.

standing.

One of the things which is sometimes a source of confusion for those whose Catholic formation took place before Vatican II is a shift in emphasis, even in official teaching, from a concern with *Christ's* sacrifice in the eucharist to a concern with the *sacrifice of the church*. At the time of the Reformation, the role of the church (i.e. of all the church, not simply the priest-celebrant) in the eucharist had faded into the background. Both piety and reflection so concentrated on the understanding of the eucharist as a representation of the sacrifice of Christ that the very forms of the ceremonial were seen as witnessing to that understanding. When the reformers, with a different understanding of the eucharist, began to change the ceremonies, it came to be seen as an attack on the nature of the eucharist as a sacrifice.

But in our own century, first scholarly reflection, and then the movement for liturgical renewal, began to recover a sense of the eucharist as sacrifice of the church.[3] Inevitably, this demanded a change in ceremonial, so that people could experience the Mass, not as something done by the priest, but as *their* offering. Most of the reforms of the rite of Mass were introduced precisely for that reason, to clarify the role of the whole church in offering the eucharist. This is strongly asserted at the beginning of the first chapter of the General Instruction on the Order of Mass:

> 1. The celebration of Mass is the action of Christ and the people of God hierarchically assembled. For both the universal and the local Church, and for each person, it is the center of the whole Christian life. The Mass reaches the high point of the action by which God in Christ sanctifies the world and the high point of men's worship of the Father, as they

[3]For a useful summary of this development before Vatican II see Charles Davis, *Liturgy and Doctrine* (New York: Sheed and Ward, 1960), 93-112. Historically, understanding of eucharistic sacrifice evolved from an understanding of the eucharist as sacrifice of the church into an understanding of the eucharist as sacrifice of Christ. See Edward Kilmartin, "Sacrificium Laudis: Content and Function of Early Eucharistic Prayers," *Theological Studies* 35 (1974) 268-287.

adore him through Christ, his Son. During the
course of the year the mysteries of redemption are
recalled at Mass so that they are in some way made
present. All other actions and works of the Christian
life are related to the eucharistic celebration, leading
up to it and flowing from it.

2.   It is of the greatest importance that the celebration of the Mass, the Lord's Supper, be so arranged
that the ministers and the faithful may take their
own proper part in it and thus gain its fruits more
fully. *For this Christ the Lord instituted the eucha-*
ristic sacrifice of his body and blood and entrusted it
to his bride, the Church, as a memorial of his pas-
sion and resurrection.

3.   The purpose will be accomplished if the celebration takes into account the nature and circumstances of each assembly and is planned to bring about
conscious, active, and full participation of the people, motivated by faith, hope, and charity. *Such*
participation of mind and body is desired by the
Church, is demanded by the nature of the celebra-
tion, and is the right and duty of Christians by
reason of their baptism.

We can note a similar function of official teaching in
relation to piety with regard to another important eucharistic doctrine, the doctrine of *transubstantiation.* As we have
already seen in relation to eucharistic sacrifice, official
teaching plays a certain kind of mediating role, correcting
some things and affirming others. The term transubstantiation first entered official Roman Catholic teaching at the
fourth Lateran Council in 1215, where it was used to describe the change by which Christ becomes present under the
forms of bread and wine. As interpreted by scholastic theology and canonized by the Council of Trent, the doctrine
treads a critical path between the possibilities of a kind of

sanctified cannibalism at one extreme, and a denial of Christ's eucharistic presence on the other.

For "transubstantiation" is a technical term which, on the one hand, asserts that the change is real, that Christ does indeed become present under the forms of bread and wine, wholly, fully, really. This is the import of insisting that the change is "substantial" — a "substantial" change means a real and actual change. On the other hand, the term asserts what is evident enough to the contemporary mind, that the appearances, or more correctly, none of the empirical properties, of bread and wine are in any way changed by consecration. For in scholastic understanding, a substantial change is a change in the inner, underlying reality of a thing. To say that "transubstantiation" occurs is simply to say that the inner underlying reality has changed.[4]

Here again, we may observe an important shift not only in piety but in official concern. As long as the church reacted defensively to what it understood as Protestant denials of Christ's eucharistic presence, there was an almost exclusive stress on Christ's presence under the forms of bread and wine. But the recovery of the understanding of the eucharist as the sacrifice of the church has included a recovery of appreciation of other modes of Christ's presence — his presence in the assembly and its prayer, his presence in the ministers of the assembly, his presence in the proclaimed word — as well as his presence under the forms of bread and wine.[5]

There can be no doubt that some of the "loss of the sense of mystery" which people have experienced is due to what we may describe as a certain "diffusion of presence." Before Vatican II, the Mass rite almost exclusively concentrated on

---

[4]Perhaps the most useful article for the beginner in technical theology on eucharistic presence is Piet Schoonenberg, "Presence and the Eucharistic Presence," *Cross Currents* 17 (1967) 39-54. For others, Joseph Powers, *Eucharistic Theology* (New York: Herder and Herder, 1968) remains a contemporary classic, as in article form is Edward Schillebeeckx' "Transubstantiation, Transignification, Transfinalization," *Worship* 40 (1966) 324-338.

[5]See Edward Kilmartin, "Christ's Presence in the Liturgy," in *Bread from Heaven*, ed. Paul Bernier (New York: Paulist Press, 1977), 102-113.

Christ's presence under the forms of bread and wine (the consecration was the "dread moment," and everything led up to it and was subordinated to it). The prizing of the role of the assembly, the enhancing of ministry by diversification (using adults other than the priest in the sanctuary), the amount of time and ceremony devoted to the Word, do all "detract" from the concentration of yesteryear. The only authentic way to a recovery of an appropriate "sense of mystery" is to prize these more neglected modes of presence, both in action and in reflection — tasks which have barely begun.

The first thing we need to recover, then, is a sense of the eucharist as a sacrifice of the church — a matter which we will now explore in the next chapter.

Recommended Reading

Tad Guzie, *Jesus and The Eucharist* (New York: Paulist Press, 1974).

Monika Hellwig, *The Meaning of the Sacraments* (Dayton: Pflaum/Standard, 1972).

Arthur Mirgeler, *Mutations of Western Christianity* (Notre Dame: University of Notre Dame Press, 1968).

David Power, "Words that Crack: The Uses of 'Sacrifice' in Eucharistic Discourse," *Worship* 53 (1979) 386-404.

CHAPTER IV

THE BREAKING OF BREAD WITH THANKSGIVING
The Eucharist of Jesus and His First Followers

In an ancient document called the Didache or Teaching of the Twelve Apostles, we find the following two accounts of the eucharist of the early Christians:

(In chapters 9 and 10)

Do the eucharist in this manner —

First, over the wine cup, "We thank you our Father, for the holy vine of David your servant which you made known to us through Jesus your servant. Glory to you into the ages. Amen."

And concerning the broken bread fragments, "We thank you our Father, for the life and knowledge which you made known to us through Jesus your servant. Glory to you into the ages. Amen."

"Even as it was scattered upon the mountains and gathered together, this broken bread became one. In this way let the church be gathered from the ends of the earth into your kingdom, for yours are the glory and power into the ages. Amen."

And let no one eat or drink from your eucharist except those baptized in the name of the Lord. For concerning this, it has come from the Lord, "Do not give that which is holy to dogs."

And when you are filled, in this way do eucharist, "We thank you, holy father, for your holy name which you made to dwell in our hearts, and for the knowledge and faith and immortality which you made known to us through Jesus your servant. Glory to you into the ages.   Amen.

You, all powerful master, created all things for the sake of your name. You gave food and drink to humankind for enjoyment, so they could give you thanks; and you graced us with the spiritual food and drink unto life eternal through Jesus your servant. Before all we thank you because you are powerful. Glory to you into the ages.   Amen.   Remember, Lord, your church: rescue it from all evil and perfect it in your love; gather it from the four winds, sanctify it and bring it into your kingdom which you have prepared for it, for yours are the power and the glory into the ages.   Amen.

Let grace come and let this world pass away. Amen.

Hosanna to the God of David.

If any are holy, let them come; if anyone is not, let them change.

Maranatha.   Amen.

And let prophets do eucharist according to their ability.

(In chapter 14)

And so when you gather on the day of the Lord, break a loaf of bread and give thanks, confessing your trespasses in order that your sacrifice might be pure. And if any are in dispute, let them not come together with you, until they are reconciled. For "in every time and place offer me pure sacrifice because I am the great king," says the Lord, "and my name is wonderful among the nations."

While it is not possible to say that these texts reflect everything about the earliest Christian practice, the description of the eucharist in Didache 9 and 10 coincides very closely with the so-called long version of the last supper account in the Gospel according to St. Luke (cf. Luke 22:17-20). There, Jesus is portrayed as first taking a cup of wine and giving thanks, then taking the bread, and finally giving thanks over a second cup of wine.

If the contemporary mind, shaped by the experience of the eucharistic prayer with its inclusion of the institution narrative (story of the last supper), resists the comparison, it may be helpful to observe that the last supper words of Jesus, "This is my body, this is my blood," are words of interpretation. The use of the words of Jesus as a formula for consecration only came as the result of a lengthy development in the church's prayer pattern. This is not to say that the early Christians did not believe in Christ's eucharistic presence. It simply means that it had not occurred to them to think of that presence as happening because of the recitation of a hallowed formula. For them, when they gave thanks over the bread and the cup, Christ was present.[1] This is why they can describe the food and drink of the eucharist as "spiritual." The original Greek actually means something much more dynamic and realistic than the term "spiritual" usually connotes in today's speech. All too often, we mean by "spiritual" a little less than real, or metaphorical. The first Christians meant precisely the opposite. Probably the Greek *pneumatikos* which is translated "spiritual" would be more vividly and truly rendered as "spirit filled," or even perhaps "divine." Certainly it means to suggest that which is dynamically associated with the divine.

Commentators have frequently noted that Jesus is often described in New Testament Last Supper narratives as ending his words with the command, "When you do this, do it as my memorial." And the command of Jesus to "Do this" is to perform the action which he performed—to take bread, give

---

[1]See Edward Kilmartin, "Sacrificium Laudis: Content and Function of Early Eucharistic Prayers," *Theological Studies* 35 (1974), 268-287.

thanks, etc.—not to say a formula.[2] In other words, that the early church understood the bread and wine to represent Jesus Christ given for us would not require that the early church used a specific formula of words within its prayer to articulate that meaning. In fact, the real problem is—how did the words of interpretation find their way into the eucharistic prayer in the first place? From the point of view of its literary genre, it is a prayer of blessing or thanksgiving, with a subordinate element of petition. The insertion of a narrative would interrupt its natural flow. Some commentators believe that the real problem is not to explain why the last supper narrative material is absent in Didache, but to explain why it became present in later eucharistic prayers.[3]

Keeping in mind that Didache 9-10 was probably developed at about the same time the books of the New Testament were being written, and perhaps represents a stage of development earlier than some of them, the lack of last supper reference may be all the more understandable. The New Testament suggests not one, but several different sorts of tradition about the origins of the eucharist in the ministry of Jesus—stories about meals with sinners, stories about the feeding of the multitude, the last supper stories, stories about meals after the resurrection. In the New Testament itself, there are distinct preferences within different traditions for preferring one set of stories over another. St. Paul, for instance, appeals to the last supper. But the Gospel according to John places the origin of the eucharist within the context of the story of the feeding of the multitude, and says nothing about the eucharist in his account of the last supper. These various traditions were not harmonized until well after the writing of the New Testament books (a process not completed until the end of the first century) and well after those books had been collected together (a process still under way in the middle of the second century). From this

[2]See Gregory Dix, *The Shape of the Liturgy* (London: Dacre Press, 1945), 48-140.

[3]Louis Ligier, "The Origins of the Eucharistic Prayer," *Studia Liturgica* 9 (1973), 161-185.

perspective, Didache 9-10 is perhaps best seen as representing the eucharist of a church which preferred to ground its eucharistic understandings in the story of the feeding of the multitude. And so instead of last supper references, the strongest references are to bread broken and shared. Rather than saying Didache 9-10 lacks an institution narrative, it is perhaps more accurate to say that it lacks a last supper institution narrative, and instead prefers a feeding of the multitude institution narrative.

Some commentators are still reluctant to see in Didache 9-10 a full eucharist. It is assumed that Didache 9-10 and Didache 14 speak of two different rites, the first an agape or minor eucharist, and the second, a sacrificial rite detached from the meal context. At first sight, Didache does lack clear reference to the dying and rising of Christ, and in view of the New Testament's association of the death and resurrection of Jesus with the eucharist, it would be difficult to defend a rite as an authentic eucharist when it failed to make such an essential connection. It is also a fact that the Didache prayers utterly lack any language of sacrifice or oblation, and in this they are very unlike later prayers known to us. Moreover, in the later (early third century) *Apostolic Tradition,* we find just such an arrangement—there is a full eucharist after the classic pattern on Sunday; it is separated from the full meal, and is complete with an institution narrative, extensive references to Christ's dying and rising (anamnesis), and offers the bread and cup in oblation. And alongside this pattern, there is a "Lord's Supper" for domestic use within a full meal context which is described by the Apostolic Tradition as *not* being a full and authentic eucharist.

Under scrutiny though, these apparent objections break down. The prayers in Didache 9-10 mention Jesus as servant (the Greek *pais,* which means both child and slave) no less than five times. This is the same term which is used of the suffering servant of Isaiah 53 in the Greek Septuagint Bible, the text which would have been known to this Greek-speaking community. In describing Jesus as God's servant, the Didache prayers show that they share the very under-standing of Jesus which underlies the Gospel passion narra-tives, St. Paul's account of the institution of the eucharist, and the eucharist story of the disciples on the road to Emmaus in the Gospel according to St. Luke.

Moreover, absence of a language of oblation within the eucharistic prayer does not mean that the eucharist was not understood sacrificially, any more than a lack of an institu-tion narrative necessarily implies lack of belief in eucharistic real presence. Sacrifice is an interpretative category. That is to say, what makes an action sacrificial is not what is done, but what the action means. And prayers may not necessarily express all the meaning that is invested in an action. The passover supper of the Jews was understood as a sacrifice too, but none of the prayers of the supper have ever con-tained any language of offering, oblation, or sacrifice.

Certainly, the text of Didache 14 could have been added at a later time, when the eucharist was separated from the common meal. But it is gratuitous to assume that the eucha-rist of Didache 14 necessarily differs from that described in Didache 9-10. To "break bread" was often first century shorthand for a full meal, a usage which is very common in the New Testament.

Moreover, the distinction between "agape" and "full eucharist" is probably anachronistic when applied to the earlier period of the church's life. It seems to be more faithful to the facts to assume that all meals of the earliest Christians eaten together (i.e. as a community of believers, and not simply as separated family households) were under-stood as eucharistic. The need for an authentic and official presider over the eucharist seems to have developed only in the face of crisis. At the turn of the second century, the need to distinguish authentic Christian assemblies from heretical groups came to the fore. The solution was to limit the authentic eucharist to that which was celebrated under the presidency of the bishop or his representative. Doubtless it was impossible to suppress the custom of gathering for sacred repasts under the presidency of those other than the bishop or his representative. A way to deal with this custom was found in the making of a distinction between the authentic bishop's eucharist and the *agape* or Lord's Supper.

In the prayer pattern of Didache 9-10, then, we may legitimately see a model of what the eucharistic celebration of the New Testament era looked like. It is that sort of event that the New Testament authors have in mind when they mention the eucharist. Clearly, for the first Christians, the mention of the word "eucharist" did not, as it often does for us, suggest a holy thing, the consecrated bread. For them, it was fundamentally a holy action, the sharing of the eucharistic meal. The New Testament's own preferred terms for the eucharist are verbs, *eucharistein,* to give thanks and praise, or *eulogein,* to bless (in the sense of praise, as in the Psalm, "Bless the Lord, O my soul"); or they speak of it as *klases ton arton,* the breaking of bread. The eucharist was not a thing: it was something done.

Nowhere in the New Testament is the eucharist actually described as a sacrifice or an oblation. But this is not exactly the same thing as the New Testament authors not ascribing a sacrificial meaning to the eucharist. For when it comes to their interpretation of what the giving of thanks and praise, or blessing, or the breaking of bread means, they do ascribe a sacrificial meaning to the event. With the sole exception of St. Paul's account in I Corinthians 11, all the New Testament last supper institution narratives describe Jesus as saying that his body/blood are given "for many," that is, for a numberless multitude. Thus the eucharist is seen as associating the participants in Christ's own sacrificial death.

The question is, then, in what sense is Christ's death understood as a sacrifice. What was the meaning of sacrifice for the New Testament authors? All of the last supper institution accounts refer to the blood of the new and everlasting covenant. The expression "blood of the covenant" is thus a comparison with the action of Christ and the covenant sacrifice of Exodus 24, which ratified the covenant at Sinai. Blood was splashed on the altar and on the people. The very language, "This is my body. . .this is my blood" indicates that Jesus is presented as the one given in sacrifice for the human race. The twin concepts of flesh (body) and blood refer to the two components of animals offered in sacrifice. In other words, in saying "this is my body. . .this is my blood," Jesus is saying, "This is myself, given in sacrifice."[4]

It is important to note, however, that in New Testament terms, the body/blood phraseology is *not* a reminiscence of the form of Christ's death (this was the contribution of medieval piety). The form of Christ's death was crucifixion, a basically bloodless death by suffocation. The body/blood language refers not to the form of Christ's death, but to its *meaning*, as the event bringing God and humankind together in reconciliation. Much of our own difficulty with appreciating the biblical language lies in our perceiving it through the filters of late medieval and reformation piety and art. That piety took the biblical image about redemption "in his blood" to refer literally to Christ's bleeding on the cross, and took the eucharistic elements to represent his crucified flesh and shed blood *en tableau*. But in biblical terms, phrases like "in his blood" or the body/blood language of the institution narratives refer, not to the literalism of physical detail, but to the significance of the event of Christ's death.

In a world where the smoke of sacrifice rose from temples in every town, the only possible way to speak of the meeting of God and humankind in reconciliation was to speak of it in the vocabulary of ritual sacrifice. The expressions "in his blood" and the body/blood language are borrowed from the vocabulary of ritual sacrifice to describe the meaning of a non-ritual event, Christ's dying and rising. And so what the institution narratives are saying, in their language of body/blood, blood of the covenant, is that Christ is the one who reconciles us to the Father, and to share in the eucharistic meal is to share in that reconciliation.

---

[4]See Joachim Jeremias, *The Eucharistic Words of Jesus* (London: SCM Press, 1966), especially 219 ff. See also Bertil Gartner, "The Eucharist as Sacrifice in the New Testament," *Lutherans and Catholics in Dialogue* III, 27-36.

It may be observed at this point that for the authors of the New Testament, there is no possible dichotomy between the eucharist as meal and the eucharist as sacrifice. To contrast them is more confusing than to contrast apples and oranges. For the New Testament writers, there is simply no problem, because the eucharist is simply a meal with sacrificial significance. To share in the eucharistic meal is to share in the sacrificial event of Christ's death.

The New Testament authors were, however, extremely careful to avoid suggesting that the eucharistic sacrifice was any sort of new ritual sacrifice.

And so, the New Testament authors are careful to dissociate the eucharist from any sort of contemporary temple sacrifice. Its frames of reference are the once and for all covenant sacrifice of Exodus 24 and the atonement sacrifice of the suffering servant of Isaiah 53:12 (". . .because he poured out his life to death, and was numbered with the transgressors, yet he bore the sins of many and made intercession for the transgressors."). The Isaian text found its place in the institution narratives' reference to Christ's gift of himself, "for many." And no passage was more important for the early church than Isaiah 52:12—53:12; it is the background of all the passion narratives. But the action of the suffering servant's action is not a ritual.

The one contemporary sacrifice which is a frame of reference for New Testament interpretation of the eucharist is the paschal meal.[5] All of the New Testament accounts of the institution of the eucharist situate it in a paschal context. For the synoptic gospels, the last supper is itself the passover meal. For St. Paul, the association is made by describing the cup as the festal cup, the "cup of blessing." And all the gospels place the eucharistic stories of the feeding of the multitude within the passover season. The biblical texts point to Christ's being understood at the new paschal lamb of sacrifice. But while in the time of Jesus the passover had to be eaten in Jerusalem because of the requirement that the

---

[5]See Max Thurian, *The Eucharistic Memorial*, 2 Vols. (Richmond: John Knox Press, 1961), Vol. II, 16ff.

lambs be slain in the temple, it was not the slaying of the lambs that was understood as sacrificial. It was the paschal *meal* that constituted the paschal sacrifice. The all important event was the eating of the meal; the slaying of the lambs in the temple was more of a rubrical nicety, a necessary preliminary to the sacrificial act, not its center. And the paschal meal was seen as relating the participants, not to the altar in Jerusalem (as would have been the case if the central point was the slaying of the lambs and the pouring of their blood on the altar), but to the exodus events of deliverance from Egypt and the making of the covenant at Sinai.

The relative lack of importance ascribed to the temple slaying of the lambs can be seen in the very different treatment of the remains of the blood and the remains of the lamb. As for the lamb which was to be eaten, there were careful requirements that it be eaten whole and entire. There had to be sufficient number to consume all of the lamb. What remained was to be carefully burned. The lamb's blood, on the other hand, was allowed to run into the brook Kidron, where it was gathered up for fertilizer!

The New Testament's concern not to associate the sacrifice of the eucharist in any direct way with temple worship is no accident. Its concern is to highlight the direct connection of the celebration of the eucharist with the living of the Christian life. The institution of the eucharist is not seen as the institution of a new ritual form, but rather, as the summation of what it means to live as a Christian. This is doubtless rooted in the centrality of table ministry in the whole ministry of Jesus, not just at the last supper, but from its very inception. The chief accusations of his enemies seem to have centered around his behavior at table—that he was too fond of eating and drinking and that he consorted at table with sinners and outcasts. Jesus' ministry at table is seen as so central in the gospel of Luke that it can say of the disciples on the road to Emmaus after the resurrection that they "recognized him in the breaking of bread." There are two strands of tradition in the New Testament last supper accounts, one which describes the meal itself, Christ's taking the bread and the cup, etc., and the other, which gives the discourses and prayers of Jesus on the implications of living out the new covenant, of living as servants of God in communion with one another. This is especially evident in the gospel of John, with its story of the washing of the disciples' feet and Christ's farewell discourses and prayers, as it is in the gospel of St. Luke, where the rebuke of the disciples who seek to be first is a central last supper story. In a masterful way, St. Paul unites the two strands of tradition, the stories of the supper and the stories of the discourses, in one powerful statement (cf. I Cor. 11:17-34).

A similar kind of tradition underlies the stories of the feeding of the multitudes. They are understood as events of Christ's care for the people: it is recorded that he "had compassion upon the multitude," and the compassionate attitude of Christ is contrasted with that of the disciples, who would have sent the crowds away.

Several New Testament texts give a prominent place to a command put on the lips of Jesus, "do this as a memorial *(eis anamnesin)* of me," a command retained in the liturgical tradition of later centuries. Much attention has been given to the meaning of the expression *eis anamnesin* (in memory, as a memorial, in commemoration, in remembrance, for the remembrance). It is generally agreed that the expression means more than simply remembering in the "subjective psychological sense." That is, it means more than remembering in the sense of "thinking about" or "meditating upon." To do something as a memorial is to make present the saving event which the action commemorates. And so "Do this in memory of me" means that when the supper is shared, those involved take part in the event of Christ's saving death. To do something as a memorial gives it the character of an oblation, an offering, for to do something "in memorial" is to do it so that *God* will "remember." A memorial is the presentation of an event of salvation history before God so as to ask for God's continuance of that history here and now and in the future. What are known technically as the *anamnesis* and the *epiclesis* of later eucharistic prayers—the sections after the institution narrative which says in effect, "We remember, we offer, we pray."—express this threefold aspect of memorial as presence of saving event, presentation of the event before God, invocation for God's present and future action.[6]

Liturgical scholarship has drawn attention to the fact that "Do this" *(touto poiete)* is essentially a "rubric" for the whole action of the supper—the taking of bread and cup, the giving of thanks over them, the breaking of the bread, the sharing of the bread and cup. But it is not simply the ritual gestures of taking, praying, sharing, that in and of themselves constitute the "this" of Jesus' command. It is those gestures as expressive of the believing community's relationship of caring and sharing which constitute them as the stuff of the memorial which is offered to God. And so the sacrificial language which the New Testament applies to the eucharist (body/blood, blood of the covenant, "for many," paschal meal) refers not simply and directly to the eating and drinking, but to that sharing in the Supper in context of a whole life pattern of loving service of one another.

It is not precisely as a meal that the eucharist is important for the New Testament. The common assertion that the eucharist originally took place within the context of an "ordinary meal" is seriously misleading. A meal sufficiently ample to be accompanied with a prayer of thanksgiving was already in Israel a deeply religious event. The blessing of the bread (in our language, more accurately described as thanksgiving for the bread) which accompanied every meal made of it an event of religious significance, a praise of God for the promised Land which provided the bread, and by implication an acknowledgement of God as both creator and covenant maker. What is unique in the accounts of Jesus' own ministry is that he took this domestic rite and made it central for the lives of his followers. During his own ministry, sharing at table was the scenario of his care for sinners, and what he bequeathed to his followers was that

---

[6]See Thurian, *loc. cit.;* also Aidan Kavanagh, "Thoughts on the Roman Anaphora," *Worship* 39 (1965), 515-529.

example of ministry. The transposition of the domestic rite into a more public context, dramatized in the stories of the feeding of the multitude, indicates that his intent was that the mark of his followers should be that the care characteristic of familial bonds should radiate outward to others.[7] All of this is charmingly depicted in St. Luke's idyllic account of the earliest days of the church:

> "The faithful all lived together and owned everything in common; they sold their goods and possessions and shared out the proceeds among themselves according to what each one needed.
> They went as a body to the Temple every day but met in their houses for the breaking of bread; they shared their food gladly and generously; they praised God and were looked up to by everyone."   Acts 2:44-47 JB

It is as a meal shared that the eucharist has its particular significance, not simply in the sharing of food, but in the sharing of food as representative of the loving service which the members of the assembly offer one another. The preoccupation with the food as shared is especially evident in the language used to describe the action of the eucharist. The bread is not simply spoken of as bread, but in the gospels as bread broken, and St. Paul refers not simply to the bread but to the one loaf. The meal aspect is radically subordinated to the central sharing of loving service.

The New Testament understanding of the eucharist is perhaps best summed up in the expression that is described as characteristic of Jesus' own table ministry — he "gave thanks." No term in English is quite adequate to translate the New Testament *eucharistein* (to "give thanks") or *eulogein* (to "bless"), for they speak for the whole understanding of eucharist which has been explored in the preceding pages. For some understanding of the meaning of "thanksgiving"

---

[7]For the integral relationship between worship and life in the New Testament, see Ferdinand Hahn, *The Worship of the Early Church* (Philadelphia: Fortress Press, 1973).

in the New Testament, it is most helpful to examine the first century eucharist as it is presented in a document from the latter part of the first century, the Didache, or *Teaching of the Twelve Apostles*. The doing of eucharist is as in the New Testament seen as the focal point of a life of mutual care and concern. Appealing to Malachi 1:11, which speaks of a pure sacrifice to be offered among the gentiles, Didache defines that sacrifice as that life of mutual concern, focused in sharing at the common table — as we saw in the citation of Didache 14 at the beginning of this chapter. The eucharist described in the Didache follows the pattern of the Jewish Sabbath or festive meal, with a first thanksgiving with wine, a kind of sacred toast of the feast, and the second thanksgiving for wine (the last of the three blessings) being the prayer over the "cup of blessing" which St. Paul mentions.

It is prayers of this type which the New Testament has in mind when it says that Jesus "gave thanks" or that he "said the blessing." They are grounded in the tradition of Jewish prayer, especially of the *berakah* or blessing (thanksgiving) prayer.[8] A *berakah* was one designed to express the totality of the community's relationship to God, e.g. "Blessed are you, Lord our God, King of the Universe," the ordinary blessing for bread at table. Here in the Didache, the familial relationship between God and his people is stressed: God is named as Father. It speaks not only for the understanding of God, but also of the relationships of those in the community one to another. To name God as Father is to acknowledge that the members of the community see one another as brothers or sisters in faith.

A second fundamental element in *berakah* is the recounting of the motives or reasons for giving thanks and praise. This is not an itemized list, but an enthusiastic ecstatic proclamation. God is the primary subject of this part of the *berakah*, as the one who is the cause of the assembly's joy and admiration, but also as the one to whom the community pledges its fidelity. He is the one who is deeply involved in

[8]See Robert Ledogar, "The Eucharistic Prayer and the Gifts over which it is Spoken," *Worship* 41 (1967) 578-596.

the life of the community, through the creation, and through his covenant with his people. The prayer begins in the immediacy of what can be seen, touched and felt, in this case, food and drink, but reaches the whole of creation and all of God's purposes.

Israel honored God as creator, and rejoiced in his creation, but its most significant experience of God was in the making of the covenant— it was the covenant which conferred its religious uniqueness. The covenant made Israel to be as a unique people.

In these Christian *berakoth*, then, it is the new covenant accomplished in Jesus that occupies the center of attention. The prayer speaks for what has been done in the past— what has been done "through your servant Jesus," i.e. through the death and resurrection of Jesus. But the covenant is present as well as past, and as such is a motive for the praise of God. God not only makes but also sustains the covenant. The "God of David" is also *this community's* God, and so the prayer speaks of the knowledge and faith and immortality which have been given through Jesus, and it petitions for the fulfillment of God's purposes for his people.

Thus to "give thanks" is not simply to express gratitude, but to speak for a relationship between God and his people, in which God is seen as involved with his people, and in which the people are seen as pledging their commitment to him and to one another. Because to "give thanks" is to affirm the relationship between God and his people, and thus on the side of his people, to express their commitment, such prayers are, as the New Testament understands eucharistic sacrifice, inherently sacrificial. By joining in this action, the assembly affirms its identification with the Jesus who gave himself, and who signified that self-gift by this breaking bread with his disciples.

Jesus' institution of the eucharist, then, does not represent the institution of a new rite. Its ritual patterns were already ancient in the domestic prayer of Israel. The uniqueness of the Christian eucharist is to be found in the transposition of that domestic ritual within the more public context of the whole believing community. It represents not a new rite, but a challenge to a new way of living. The whole point of the transposition was that the loving service and hospitality characteristic of domestic life was to be the characteristic of the whole Christian community.

Enthusiasts for heightening the meal aspect of eucharist (e.g. with altar breads that look more like real bread) might well ponder that the issue for the New Testament is not any such sort of ritual nicety, but the quality of shared life among those who participate together in the eucharist. There is everything to be said for the end of the obsessive ritualistic fussiness that has been characteristic of Catholic worship for centuries. But the task is not to replace a fussy ritual with one which is not so fussy. The task is to enable the development of the kind of Christian community where a communal rite can speak for common responsibility and common caring.

Against the background of the New Testament, then, the understanding of the eucharist as meal or thanksgiving is distorted if it in any way waters down a sense of the sacrificial character of the eucharist, or if joyous celebration is taken to exclude a sober sense of making and expressing a commitment. For the first Christians, there was no disjunction between meal and sacrifice, the seriousness of the Christian commitment and the joy of their hope.

And that integral sense of the eucharist survived into subsequent generations. How much the eucharistic thanksgiving had to do with expressing the seriousness of the Christian commitment can be seen in the following prayer which survives from the age of martyrdom (and in edited form, appears as Eucharistic Prayer II of the Roman Sacramentary, Eucharistic Prayer B of Rite II of the Book of Common Prayer of the Episcopal Church in the United States, and Eucharistic Prayer 4 of the Lutheran Service Book). This eucharistic prayer appears in the *Apostolic Tradition* attributed to Hippolytus of Rome.

Eucharistic Prayer of the Apostolic Tradition

We give you thanks, O God, through your beloved child Jesus Christ, whom in the last times you sent to us as savior and redeemer, the messenger of your will.

He is your inseparable Word, through whom you made all things, and who was well-pleasing to you.

You sent him from heaven into the womb of a virgin. Having dwelt in the womb, he was made flesh, and was manifest as your Son, born of the Holy Spirit and the Virgin.

He fulfilled your will, acquiring a holy people for you, stretching out his hands to suffering, to free by his passion those who trusted in you.

When he was handed over to voluntary suffering, to crush death and break the chains of the devil, tread hell under foot and enlighten the righteous, establish the bonds and manifest the resurrection, taking bread, giving you thanks, he said, "Take, eat, this is my body which will be broken for you." Likewise the cup, saying, "This is my blood which is poured out for you; when you do this, you make my memorial."

Therefore, calling to mind his death and resurrection, we offer you the bread and the cup, thanking you for counting us worthy to stand before you and serve you.

And so we ask you to send your Holy Spirit on the offering of holy church, gathering us into one, granting to all who receive the holy gifts to be filled with the Holy Spirit for the building up of faith in truth, so that we may praise you and glorify you through your child Jesus Christ, through whom be glory and honor to you, to the Father and the Son with the Holy Spirit in the holy church, now and for ages unending.   Amen.

The prayer unfolds as a thanksgiving for Jesus Christ, God's servant and messenger who comes into the world to conquer Satan and win for God a holy people. The prayer crescendoes to the line, "stretching forth his hands upon the cross," highlighting Christ's role as obedient servant. When this prayer was actually in use, the whole assembly stood to pray with hands outstretched and raised up, so that with the prayer's operative line speaking of the present, "thanking you for counting us worthy to stand in your presence and serve you," the prayer dramatically identified the assembled congregation with Christ the servant. To describe the eucharist as "praise and thanksgiving" is not to water down the notion of sacrifice, but to affirm, with the General Instruction on the Order of Mass, that "the meaning of the eucharistic prayer is that the whole assembly offers the sacrifice." (#54, General Instruction on the Order of Mass)

Recommended Reading

Bread from Heaven, ed. Paul Bernier (New York: Paulist Press, 1977).

Deiss, Lucien, *It is the Lord's Supper* (New York: Paulist Press, 1975).

Rouillard, Phillippe, "From Human Meal to Christian Eucharist," *Worship* 52 (1978) 425-439.

CHAPTER V

ONE BREAD, ONE BODY
Liturgical Needs
Today and Tomorrow

It is sometimes assumed that our liturgy lacks power because its fundamental symbols have ceased to have relevance. This may be true of certain secondary symbols — the use of candles for instance. In a world of electric light, a candlelight service could be nothing but a sentimental piece of religious escapism. Yet this is not so when it comes to the primary eucharistic symbols — bread and wine, body, blood. Here, at least potentially, are the primary preoccupations of post-scientific era. Bread and wine, we may note, are the products of technology. As such, they speak for human art and skill, for a humanity called to build a city in this world. Body and blood speak robustly both for the life of the heart and senses, as they do for mortality and dying. At least in possibility, the eucharistic symbols do speak for the world of love and work, struggle and prayer that is the real substance of the life of faith. From this perspective, there is everything to be said for a more robustly sensuous experience of eucharistic celebration, with the use of real bakery bread and good commercial wine as the normal, rather than the exceptional practice. Similarly, there is everything to be said for gracious gestures, generous furnishing, and festive ornament in the event of worship. These things all pertain to the art of hospitality which is the central value of the eucharist. How else shall we speak of the One who calls from within our midst to share the life of God among us?

Yet all of these things make no sense except as natural and common sense manifestations of a deeper conviction — that the eucharist is integrally connected to the daily living of the Christian life in this world. The contemporary experience of God demands that we see that living as a common task shared with one another. If God is named primarily in dialogue, then God is most to be found in communion with one another.

There is in fact a certain Christian imperative to be attentive to these things as never before. Our world is for better or worse a human world, a world filled with artifacts which remove us from nature. Between us and nature stand the works of our own hands, even if we are farmers. The direct communion with the earth and with growing things, the fellowship with animals that were the privileges of our ancestors are ours no longer, and can at best be fleeting luxuries or the prerogatives of tiny minorities. We have become so preoccupied with the dangers of runaway technology that we fail to reflect that the mission of God in the world is to redeem the human condition. And if we are the agents of that mission, this includes the redemption of a technological world.

Liturgical action, then, needs to speak for a befriending and taming of technology, not a rejection of it. Some sense of what that means is evoked in the book *Zen and the Art of Motorcycle Maintenance:*

> Clichés and stereotypes such as "beatnik" or "hippie" have been invented for the antitechnologists, the antisystem people, and will continue to be. But one does not convert individuals into mass people with the simple coining of a mass term. John and Sylvia are not mass people and neither are most of the others going their way. It is against being a mass person that they seem to be revolting. And they feel

that technology has got a lot to do with the forces
that are trying to turn them into mass people and
they don't like it. So far it's still mostly a passive
resistance, flights into the rural areas when they are
possible and things like that, but it doesn't always
have to be this passive.

I disagree with them about cycle maintenance,
but not because I am out of sympathy with their
feelings about technology. I just think that their
flight from and hatred of technology is self-defeat-
ing. The Buddha, the Godhead, resides quite as
comfortably in the circuits of a digital computer or
the gears of a cycle transmission as he does at the top
of a mountain or in the petals of a flower. To think
otherwise is to demean the Buddha — which is to
demean oneself.[1]

But what might this mean liturgically? It would mean, for
beginnings, the use of the best a technological culture can
supply — the use of the kind of good table wine that can be
found now at any supermarket, not romanticized and escapist homemade bread, but robust baker's bread. It would
mean the crafting of buildings, furniture and ornaments, not
according to some romantic criterion as to what ought to
look like it used to in a church, but according to a realistic
criterion as to what is practical and pleasing in its use. It
would mean that the use of recorded music would be normal
rather than exceptional, as it would mean that any use of the
"artificial" would be judged by its appropriateness for the
event rather than according to extraneous criteria of
propriety.

The hazards of technology would find their proper criticism in the cherishing of the individual. Perhaps the greatest
hazard of technology is the allowing of machines to control
our lives and our destinies. An authentic contemporary
liturgy would include a vigilance against this sort of mass

[1]Robert M. Persig, *Zen and the Art of Motorcycle Maintenance* (New York:
Bantam Books, 1974), pp. 17, 18.

culture, and would not allow itself to be shaped as it is for instance by the tyranny of mass produced leaflet missals. Thus a church which had truly found a place in the contemporary world would cherish the work of local artists, so that each individual church building and each individual act of worship had its own distinctive character.

People in our culture also suffer acute sensory deprivation, a deprivation which can only be appreciated by those who have lived with the sights and sounds and smells and changing rhythms of moisture and temperature of rural or sea life. The coming of rock music and the sexual revolution speak for that terrible need for a richer sensory experience. A greater human warmth in worship becomes a necessity. For in a technological world, the church must be a zone of healing and welcome. Many conventions of worship we have inherited from the past are not only unnecessary, they in fact endanger the authenticity of worship. A culture which lived in relative closeness to nature, in both its beauty and its horror could well afford to conduct its worship with all the conventions of chivalry. Now, the maintenance of the relics of these conventions tends to the dehumanization of worship.

Our real problem with eucharistic celebration is not its separation from the context of the meal — St Paul already made that clear in the fifties of the first Christian century. Our real problem is that the experience of eucharist has often become detached from the experience of Christian community. What the authors of the first and second century of our era strove to protect was the eucharist's proper context as an event of mutual care and concern. Liturgical reform has only laid bare a longstanding problem. If the newer gestures — the exchange of the peace, and all the other gestures of caring — are an affront, they well might be. All too often, they have too little connection with life as it is actually lived by the worshipping congregation. In this sense, the newer gestures of caring and sharing invested in the liturgy can be as profoundly alienating as the older gestures which distanced people from one another and from

God.

Unfortunately, our image of what this kind of sharing might involve all too often works from a romantic image of the eucharist which is as sentimental and inaccurate as any of the devotional syrup of years past. I refer to the all too common assumption that the ideal eucharist is a celebration of the totally committed and likeminded, or to the assumption that the eucharist of semi-strangers in the parish church is somehow necessarily "deficient." So from the liturgically minded we hear thunderings about the need for "converted" (whatever that might be) communities of faith, or we hear whinings that "you can't have community with a bunch of strangers." Jesus and the earliest Christians seem to have been of another mind altogether on the subject. One may assume that the five thousand at the feeding of the multitude did not know one another intimately, as, on the other side, we may observe that St. Luke portrays the last supper as filled with strife among the disciples as to who was the greatest among them.

We are frequently told that "lack of a sense of community" is a major liturgical problem. Yet the kind of sharing that is inherent in the eucharist of Jesus does not necessarily require a community of intimacy. If we take the model of the feeding of the multitude seriously, the suggestion is that even the tiny early communities viewed the eucharist as opening out into something like today's large parish gathering. It is not so much a lack of a sense of community as a lack of a sense of focus of common commitment that is the liturgical problem. A liturgy that is authentic by biblical standards is a eucharist celebration by a community whose investments in the care of others are real and tangible. This is a traditional theological principle, not a desirable extra. According to scholastic theology, *sacramenta significando efficiunt:* sacraments have their effect in people by being significant to them. That is to say, we cannot speak of an event being a sacrament unless it speaks for a faith lived and acted out. This is basic to the traditional teaching that sacraments are signs of faith. It is essential, then, that the eucharistic community be a community of commitment. This does not, of course, mean that each and every single member of that community has to be a stellar example of faith lived. It simply means that the community be a sufficient pool of serious commitment that it can be experienced as characteristic of the church's life. In the recent past, this was achieved by the parochial commitment to its school. With its staff of sisters and the care that others invested in it, the parish could be genuinely experienced as a center where the Christian commitment was lived out. Unfortunately, the parochial school has disappeared as a focus. Also its emphasis on the care of our own had led to a certain sectarianism.

We frequently talk in terms of a model of community that flies in the face of Catholic tradition. The writers of the gospels place the feeding of the multitude in the context of the healing of the sick, and the accounts of the last supper are, as we have seen, preoccupied with the church's role as a community of service. So, too, the great scandal of Jesus' ministry was that it opened outward from his table to the care of the outcast and the sinner. There is thus an unavoidable connection between the celebration of the eucharist and the service of human need. But the present problem is not directly one of Christian community. It is the problem, rather, of being at the service of human community. The church always supplies for the human community what the world cannot give, and this is a significant part of its mission. We can see this as already taken for granted in the gospels — part of Jesus' ministry is the healing of the sick, the supplying of what the world has failed to give. In succeeding centuries, the principle was still there: the care of widows and orphans was a central part of the concern of the church in the age of persecution. When the age of persecution ended, the desperate need for the world was for order in the world where civilization was collapsing, and the church supplied that. All through its history the church has supplied goods and services of one sort or another, depending upon the need of the world at any given time. Immigrant

Catholicism provided any number of such services for people cast adrift in an alien world — everything from the sustaining of ethnic identity to help with the forming of unions.

The desperate need of our own time is not so much goods and services — in many cases, other agencies tend to provide those. Rather, the need is often for simple human community. If the family is in trouble, it is because it is less and less surrounded by near family and helping neighbors, and more and more imploded in upon itself. If interest in politics is lacking, it is because of the disappearance of groups of common interest on a manageable scale where people feel that they can have their say. If the preaching of social justice is a problem, it is because there is no grouping of people in common care on a human scale where ordinary people can find a place. The disappearance of the neighborhood is perhaps one of the most serious social problems of our time. A neighbor is not simply somebody who is physically juxtaposed to me. A neighbor is one who is "nigh," that is, near to me, one with whom I have human bonds, not on the basis of some special interest, but on the basis of our common humanity as we live together. The fragmentation of the church into interest groups, from Dignity and Marriage Encounter to charismatic renewal is a sad mirror of secular culture, and reflects that breakdown of human community as it impinges upon the life of the church. It is a fact of parish life that often there can be virtually no sense of real human belonging without joining a special interest group.

And so if our eucharistic celebration is to have any sense of authenticity (and remembering that the liturgy speaks of community in terms of a community of service), the building of human community becomes a real priority for the assembly that celebrates the eucharist. And the only qualification for membership in that human community is to be a human being, not faith, not morals, and not ritual practice. In a city parish, then, the building up of neighborhoods as a real human community becomes the first priority for the community that celebrates the eucharist.

The eucharist is properly understood as the supper of the disciples of the Lord, the supper for those who have come to follow Jesus. The eucharist therefore has everything to do with baptism, which makes us followers of Jesus. What effect baptism *could* have on eucharistic celebration can be seen from an examination of early Christian evidence. The church's primary concern about baptism was for the baptism of adults, and a large portion of its ordinary life revolved around the preparation of new Christians for baptism. The baptism of an adult was not seen as an unusual or extraordinary thing, but rather, was one of the major tasks of the church. Baptism was preceded by lengthy preparation, normally about three years. The major purpose of that preparation was seen as the learning of a new way of life, learning to live as a Christian, the hallmark of which was the care of those of the household of faith. And so just before the final preparations for baptism, they were examined as to their way of life. Baptism did not only involve taking on a set of beliefs: it also involved a radical change in what we call lifestyle, as it involved living in close daily relationship to a new community of people. Baptism also *cost*. In an age of persecution, it was at least socially unacceptable, and potentially dangerous to one's life to become a Christian. To accept baptism was to accept the distinct possibility of martyrdom. The actual moment of baptism and first eucharist was a moment of high ritual drama. On Easter eve, the church gathered to keep vigil, not the little cut-down service we have now, but an all night watch of readings and prayers. Toward dawn, a prayer of blessing was said over the baptismal water, and the candidates were taken out to the baptismal pool, where they were baptized by immersion, naked. When they had been anointed and clothed with white robes, they were brought back in, into the midst of the congregation. After the bishop had again laid hands on them and anointed them with perfumed oil, they were given the peace (then an embrace and a real kiss), and joined for the first time in the prayer of the faithful and the eucharist which followed. In keeping with the lavishness of the rite, communion consisted not only of the ordinary eucharistic bread and wine, but also of cups of water and milk and honey, probably a relic of earlier days when the eucharist was part of a full meal.

This lavish and robustly physical celebration contrasts starkly with the account the same document gives of ordination at that time. It can take place on any ordinary Sunday, and consists in a simple prayer and laying on of hands just before the preparation of the eucharistic table. The ordination of a bishop could have taken no longer than five minutes within the course of an otherwise very ordinary eucharist. The admission of the laity to the eucharistic table, on the other hand, required three years of preparation, three days of fasting and a night of prayer by the whole church, and its ceremonies took hours. We may perhaps best understand the differences between the ancient church and the contemporary if we reflect that the first eucharistic vestments were worn by the laity — the white baptismal robes. The clergy of this period presided in the ordinary clothing of the day.

And because of its intimate connection with baptism, every eucharist was a reminder of what it meant to be a baptized Christian, a reaffirmation of the commitment of the newly baptized. The elaborate ritual leading into the first eucharist of the newly baptized reflects the way in which the church of the time prized the dedication of ordinary Christian life as the sum and substance of the whole life of the church. We have already seen that earlier in the New Testament, the connection between that life of service and the celebration of the eucharist was seen as a connection that was basic to the early Christian understanding of the eucharist. Likewise, the ordinary daily living of the Christian life came to be seen as a sacrificial offering, as the eucharist summed up that life of offering.

It is too frequently assumed that the problem of our time is infant baptism — that it opens the door to there being so many uncommitted and half-hearted adult believers. This is again a sectarian assumption. A scan of the New Testament letters makes it very clear that adult baptism is no hedge on lack of commitment. Even in the first fervor of its youth, the church found its new adult members indulging in all the vileness and pettiness that people are capable of indulging today. In any case, if God is seen as present within the world, and present to unconscious and "useless" life, there is every good cause for baptizing infants as the revelation of that divine presence. To insist on the exclusive baptism of the adults tends in our culture to feed the assumption that only those who are "useful" and conscious are worthy of attention.

The problem is not infant baptism but that baptism makes no discernible difference in the lives of so many people. Yet present preoccupations with "standards" for admitting either the children of believers or adults have become a problem too. The danger is of making certain programs and practices rather than the living of the gospel the norm for the life of a baptized person. While nothing can guarantee a life of commitment on the part of baptized people, the gospel's own standard for the life of the baptized needs to be taken seriously. That concrete standard of church life is not, as is often mistakenly supposed, "love." Only God can judge us on love, for it is a quality of acting, not any given action or set of actions, as it can only be lived out in a lifetime. This is why St. Paul gives us so many different descriptions of love in his hymn (cf. I Corinthians 13 ff), but never tells us exactly what it is. What the church can assess is the primary virtue enjoined on Christians, that which can be outwardly seen, and in which people most truly "imitate" Jesus—the virtue of hospitality. Again and again the New Testament epistles end with exhortations to hospitality, to the simple care of one another—in contemporary terms, with exhortations to neighborliness in the true and serious sense. In fact, as the New Testament epistles understand Christian morality, the issue is that central virtue of hospitality. All other moral issues are seen as subordinate to it: other moral rules are intended simply to facilitate the care of one another that is made practical in the gestures of hospitality. The ancient Apostolic Tradition asks of candi-

dates for baptism not how much they know of their catechism, or what they believe, or what their morals are, but
simply, "have they lived honestly, honored (i.e. supported)
the widows, visited the sick?"

All of this suggests an appropriate norm for the admission of either adult candidates or for the parents of children
who wish their baptism: the living out of the virtue of
hospitality in concrete commitments to the building of
human community on a human scale. This provides a discernible public way of scrutiny without the obnoxious or
irrelevant invoking of criteria of morality, ritual, or belief.
The baptismal creed, we too readily forget, is not so much a
statement of belief as the voicing of a stance. To say that one
believes in God the Father, maker of heaven and earth is to
say that one believes in one's own goodness and that of
others, and hopes for the destiny of the human race. To say
that one believes in Jesus and the Holy Spirit is to commit
oneself to living in active dialogue with the community
which claims discipleship with Jesus and communion in the
Holy Spirit. Anyone who agrees to live by the virtue of
hospitality and to worship with the household of faith has
agreed to those affirmations.

It is within this context that the future of religious community needs to be understood. From the earliest days there
have been smaller groupings within the wider Christian
community which have functioned as special centers of
witness and service. The letters of St. Paul already single out
these special communities, e.g., in the second letter to
Timothy we find: "greetings to Prisca and Aquila, and the
household of Onesiphorus." Obviously these households
have a special place in the local church, or they would not be
so singled out. In later centuries these groupings would be
monastic communities, and later yet, religious orders and
confraternities. There seems to be a surge of lay interest in
this sort of community life, even as religious communities in
the conventional sense are less and less attractive to new
candidates. These communities are important indeed, but
they are not to be seen as the future of the church unless they

remain linked both to the wider Christian community of
parish and to the building of human community in the
world.

In another sense, however, such small communities are
absolutely critical to the function of Christian community.
They are not some sort of luxury, but a necessity. The stories
of the feeding of the multitude tell us that Jesus' followers
were divided into groups of fifty. The suggestion is that
religious community is only manageable and viable when it
operates on a human scale. Our vast parishes certainly need
this kind of breaking down into groups. The very action of
the liturgy, with all its gestures of caring, presses the issue.
No doubt, one of the well-nigh intolerable tensions at the
present time is a set of liturgical gestures which speak for
dialogue in faith and a style of parish life which militates
against it.

It is against this background that the lesser ritual needs
should be seen. If the church becomes more serious about its
dialogue with the world, and works to build community
with it and within it, a more robust ceremonial and more
serious attention to liturgical art will seem only natural. Our
ceremonies, our buildings, our furnishings and our ornaments tend to be plastic or sentimental simply as a reflection
of the way we are — disconnected from the real life of real
people. If our churches have become cluttered with throwa-
way art and cheapened with poor music, it is because so
often we have not sought to build the kind of communities
of caring that are at the heart and center of its life. We have
conventionally referred to the consecrated eucharistic bread
as the "host." In a world dying for want of community and
in a church whose mission is hospitality, the word could
take on all manner of new dimensions.

Recommended Reading

Crichton, J.D., *The Once and Future Liturgy* (New York: Paulist Press, 1977).

Gelineau, Joseph, *The Liturgy Today and Tomorrow* (New York: Paulist Press, 1978).

Hovda, Robert, *Dry Bones* (Washington: The Liturgical Conference, 1973).

CHAPTER VI

TO REMEMBER THE LORD
Toward an Authentic Recovery of Liturgical Tradition

If there is a need to find a new way of living Christian community, we need equally to recover the power inherent in our panoply of ritual, not by a flight into the forms of the past, but by plumbing the depth of our most basic gestures and our most fundamental and earthy sacramental signs. For it is through those signs that we "remember" the Lord. An investment in remembering is in fact one of the most obvious features of liturgical prayer. "Do this in memory of me" sums up not only Jesus' words over the bread and wine, but also his whole intent in instituting the eucharist, and the church's whole understanding of what it means to do eucharist. Remembering, the church's recalling of its Lord and God, and its calling God to remembrance, is the fundamental root not only of the eucharist but of all Christian prayer and sacraments. It is the reason for the official insistence on the primacy of the scriptures in liturgical reading: without its memory as a people, the church is less than Christian in prayer. Likewise, the language of liturgical prayer is the language of scripture, not "neat" or literally, but echoing the history of God's people as it has come to us through the sacred writing. And there has always been a fundamental reserve about the use of sacramental elements not found in scripture. Bread and wine and oil do not appear in constant

Catholic usage because they are equally suitable to all cultures or because they are found in them. Rather, they are used because of their original use in a particular culture, that which gave birth to Christianity and which was the cradle of its history. Bread and wine and oil are instruments of communal memory, as is the specific way we use water in Christian rite.

But just what does it mean to say that when we celebrate the eucharist we do this "in memory" of Jesus? What does it mean to "remember" the crossing of the Red Sea at the paschal vigil? For we have not met the Lord as he was in the days of his mortal flesh, nor have we traveled literally from Egypt to the promised land. Theological and historical commentary has stressed the fact that liturgical remembering has to do with *God's* remembering — that when the church celebrates its sacraments, God acts in, for, and through the participants. Contemporary theological study of the nature of liturgical remembrance, both in the scriptures and in the understanding of early church fathers gives new grounding to an old teaching, that the sacraments happen *ex opere operato* — which is simply to assert that when the church gathers in faith to celebrate a sacrament, it really happens. In this way, theological reflection has stressed that sacramental remembering is not "merely subjective," i.e. is not merely a thinking about the past. Sacramental action is not merely a kind of sacred tableau of the events of salvation, but is a genuine re-living of those events. In the words of the Council of Trent, a sacrament is not simply a *nudum signum,* a bare sign.[1]

It is not simply God, however, who is the remembering subject of liturgical and sacramental prayer. Our blessings (in the eucharist, the eucharistic prayer; at baptism, the blessing of the font) which accompany sacramental action speak emphatically of *ourselves* remembering. God remembers because the church remembers, or better, when the

---

[1]For a full study of the meaning of memorial or remembering, see Max Thurian's *The Eucharistic Memorial,* (cited in Chapter IV), or Gregory Dix's *The Shape of the Liturgy,* 242 ff.

church remembers, it is then that God is acting in the church.

Thanks to recent studies on the nature of ritual, it is possible to give an intelligent account of just what are the human elements in the event of liturgical remembering. And through understanding those human elements, it is possible to come to a deeper appreciation of our sacramental signs, as it becomes possible to provide a more adequate critique of our liturgical practice, along with enabling us to plan liturgical celebration more intelligently.

Let us begin by observing some of the features of the simplest of sacramental gestures, the lighting of the new fire at the paschal vigil. Assuming that it takes place as it ought, i.e. well into the night, and out of doors in full darkness in front of the church, a variety of chords are struck in us. This is a relatively simple liturgical gesture (what in the old terminology we called a "sacramental"), yet it draws to itself a rich variety of human response. As an action, it is a mere matter of people gathering around a little knot of ministers, the priest's lighting of a small bonfire, and then the preparation of the paschal candle, with the proclamation "Jesus Christ yesterday, today, and forever. He is the Alpha and the Omega. His are the seasons and the ages."

The Primal: The Sense of Identification

But for all the simplicity of this little ceremony, it touches the human spirit at a variety of levels. At its very depth, it calls to the human experiences we all share, birth, sleeping and waking. The passage from darkness to light is one of the most basic of all human experiences: it is the passage with which we begin our lives, and it is repeated daily in our sleeping and our waking. This is not to say that such moments are *consciously* recalled in the paschal vigil: as with all good ritual events, such memories remain on the horizon of our experience: they condition the immediate perception and appreciation of what is happening in the ritual moment, without our adverting directly to them. This is perhaps clearer if we advert to another layer of experience to which the vigil calls. The keeping of a high vigil and the lighting of a fire call to all our myriad experiences of being in darkness and the moments which have involved us in light and warmth, hearth and home. Both dread and discomfort ("But it's so *long!*"), joy and anticipation are evoked by the juxtaposition of firelight with the darkness of a spring night. At the heart of this event, then, our most primitive depths are touched, harking back to birth and early infancy, and to the beginnings of childhood entirely lost to conscious memory. Good ritual, as this one is, has first of all what we may call a *primal* layer, that which speaks to our earliest and most basic experiences of life. It is by appealing to this primitive depth that symbolic forms are able to reach across the differences of individual histories and special circumstances: insofar as they touch fundamental human experiences, they can be shared, just as they can serve to unite people of diverse background and perspective. It is not true that symbols "speak for themselves," as some have asserted. Symbols only speak to us to the extent that they resonate with our experience. They seem to "speak for themselves" because they do not normally resonate consciously with prior experience, at least not immediately and obviously.

The Social and the Presocial: The Sense of Community

Besides appealing to what can be called the primal, a good ritual also appeals to what are best described as the presocial and the social, the set of experiences whereby we have learned to relate to others and found our place together with them in the world. The ceremony of the lighting of the new fire plays vigorously on this set. If the ceremony is done well, people do not take their ordinary place in church, but are called upon to assemble in the dark. The usual manners of entry into the church are purposely (and purposefully) disrupted. From the moment of stubbing one's fingers in the empty holy water font to the unfamiliarity of standing crowded on the church steps, one is compelled to relive all the moments of uncertainty about one's place with others that is inherent in new beginnings. But then, too, the assembly's finding itself together and united in the watching of the lighting of the new fire calls to the sense of wonder, surprise, and satisfaction that attends the resolution of crises of new beginnings. We experience something of a coming home, a sense of being in place, a sense of shared well-being. It is for this reason that the abandonment of flint and steel for the starting of the fire is something of a serious loss. The congregation is relieved of the tension of uncertainty — and therefore of a sense of sharing in their clergy's success when the fire is finally kindled.

It must be noted that the primal, the pre-social and the social are only touched vividly when symbolic forms are used in their full vigor. A preoccupation with convenience considerably deadens the effect of the ritual. The sense of warmth and welcome intended in the very structure of the ritual can only be appreciated to the extent that it is experienced as a passage from cold and darkness to light, comfort, and being together. The abandonment of fasting and a variety of other pre-Vatican II practices has anaesthetized us into the assumption that there is something wrong with liturgy if we experience discomfort. This is a peculiar assumption for people who claim that the supreme human act of worship took the form of a public execution. It is in fact of the essence of celebration that there be a tension between the ordeal of preparation and the comfort of festivity. It is by reducing liturgical tension (abandoning fasts, truncating vigils, lighting fire inside while the people take their ordinary places in the church, etc.) that the liturgy loses its intended connection with real and ordinary life. Doubtless, this is one of the major reasons that the liturgy is described by the young as "boring." Boredom is not caused by repetition, and it is not caused by things taking a long time. Both repetition and taking a long time are inherent in true acts of festivity. What makes something boring is our being forced to give close attention to the trivial: this is why assembly line work is boring. It is not because it takes all day or because things are done over and over that the assembly line worker is bored. The same worker is perfectly capable of watching a day of football games without boredom. It is the triviality of putting the same bolts together time after time after time that is boring, the triviality of an action which includes no tense and uncertain beginning, and therefore no satisfactory resolution. The football game is exciting precisely because it is not known who will be the winner, or how. A vigil without the tension of anticipation being heightened and enhanced runs the serious risk of trivializing its most fundamental message.

In many ways, it is the evocation of the primal, the pre-social and the social that allows a rite to "speak" to the participant, which allows the participant to enter into the event. The sense of connection with "real life," i.e. life outside of the ritual is not evoked primarily by a conscious attention by way of reflection, but by the resemblance between previously repeated experience and the ritual experience. The participant relives the feelings associated with the previous events of "real life," and therefore senses a connection between life and worship.[2] It is here, too, that a "sense of community" arises in the experience of liturgy. It is not true that the worship of pre-Vatican II Catholicism lacked a "sense of community." It in fact included a very strong sense of community, precisely because its rites allowed the common experience of tension and its resolution in festivity, especially through the keeping of fasts, but

---

[2]See the text of Karl Rahner cited on p. 142 in Chapter VIII. It is precisely this sort of experience which is evoked in liturgical memorial when sacramental signs are used in their fullness. To "remember the Lord" is not to remember an event in past time as we would, for example, in viewing a film representation of an historical event, but to remember those events in our own lives which bear the shape of the experience of Jesus Christ in the Spirit.

also through the use of archaic (and therefore time-consuming and inconvenient) ceremony. It was indeed a different sort of sense of community than we seek nowadays (a point to be explored in subsequent chapters), but it was nonetheless real. People had a deep sense of belonging and a strong sense of Catholic identity — a "sense of community" by very definition. The sense of community is sustained precisely through the sharing of trial and triumph, ordeal and festivity. To the extent that the experience of rite is faithful to life, then, it will indeed create a sense of community.

The Formally Social: The Sense of the Sacred

To return to the center of our reflection, the ceremony of the lighting of the new fire, we can observe that two sorts of experience normally and regularly attend such an event. As people gather to watch the ceremony itself, with their attention focused on the ministers and the priest's lighting of the fire, they are often struck with a sense of awe and wonder. Yet not infrequently, there are opposite reactions: a sense that the ministers look like a crowd of druids or Macbeth's witches gathered around their cauldron. There are awe and wonder, but also a vague dread and hilarity — the gamut of emotions not only most appropriate to true celebration, but also those emotions most directly and deeply associated with worship — with a "sense of mystery." We may note that these emotions are aroused most deeply at the point where the event shapes itself in the *formally social* — the point where the action is focused in the ministers' doing of something for the assembly. To speak descriptively in terms of the human experience of what happens at the level of the formally social, we may observe that it simply involves the dramatic doing of ordinary and primitive human gestures. It has been observed often enough that the Christian sacraments involve the most ordinary of gestures — bathing, dining, touching. What is not observed so frequently, and which is of equal import, is that they do not involve *mere* gestures of bathing, dining, or touching, but rather that they involve these things done in a dramatic way. In liturgical action, there are no walks, but only processions, no handing over, but only presentations, no mere feeding but gracious gestures of dining, including the preparation of the table and appreciation of the food — preparation of the altar and gifts (offertory); the formal admiring of the host and guest of honor (being one and the same — God in his Christ through the Holy Spirit) — eucharistic prayer; and carefully mannered serving — the communion rite. And it is to the extent that these gestures are carried out dramatically and carefully that they evoke the "sense of mystery." It is by ordered and dramatic ceremony that we experience the sacred. A dinky fire in a carefully enclosed pot in the church vestibule rapidly and furtively lit will call forth neither awe and wonder nor dread and hilarity, but only a sense that the time could be spent better engaged in other pursuits.

It is only when the assembly has been gathered, and when the ministers have entered into their task, that a word is proclaimed that sums up the event: "Jesus Christ yesterday, today, and forever." Rising as it does out of a community which has been attuned to the whole of each individual's experience of trial and comfort (and therefore of sin and grace), the word announced in proclamation and praise serves to sum up the event. The Lord is remembered, not as a figure from past time, but as One present to the whole of life, a present One honored in this assembly. Not unnaturally, the liturgy can then proceed to the lighting of the candles and to the paschal Exultet: a community so prepared is indeed ready for celebration. This level of *word* interprets the event, names its meaning, calls to its deepest reality. But we may note that we only hear that word effectively to the extent that other layers of our experience have been touched. The joyous hearing of the word requires a people prepared by the sense that it touches their whole lives.[3]

In terms of human experience, then, the kind of remembering that takes place in the liturgy involves the evocation of ordinary and basic experience through the use of symbolic forms and gestures (ritual) which evoke the sets of feelings associated with those experiences. This indeed involves "psychology" and "group dynamics," but not indeed those of a manipulative kind. The participants are left free to experience themselves and the event in all their own individual reality. It is precisely their rich multivalence that makes symbols to be symbols: they evoke not simply one sort of feeling, or one kind of mood, but a whole spectrum of experience. They touch the whole range of possible human response. Thus it does not matter that staying up late at night is one person's idea of a good time and another's idea of an ordeal. Ordeal and festivity are both common elements of a real vigil (remember, the word vigil simply means night watch or wake), and the symbols of the paschal vigil "work" precisely because they can touch those varied ranges of feeling and experience, as they allow for the sharing of such experience. But in the kind of ritual act we call liturgy, those basic human experiences are conjoined with proclamation and prayer which speaks of another and larger history, that of God's dealings with his people, focused in the story of one man, Jesus of Nazareth, whom we honor as incarnating God's presence among us. Liturgical remembering involves the conjunction of my conscious remembering, but the imprint of all my past that lies within me with the memory of the community focused in its scriptures and summed up in its prayer. To remember liturgically is to find ourselves identified with the biblical story. It is for this reason that the Constitution on the Liturgy and

---

[3]In its original cultural context, the ceremony of the lighting of the new fire possessed even more evocative power than it can now. When graveyards were in the front of the church building, and weddings were celebrated on the church porch (as they were in the middle ages) and when the church building was a center of civil, social, and economic as well as religious life, the lighting of the new fire over the center of life itself had to be an event of staggering power.

the General Instruction on the Order of Mass speak of the goal of "full and active participation of mind and *body*." Bodies participate in actions only by feeling and sensing and doing. And so the experience of the worshippers has everything to do with their making a full and authentic response to Jesus' command to "Do this in memory of me." It is only by liturgical action which vigorously touches the primal, the pre-social, and the social that the liturgy communicates a sense of belonging and identification, and therefore of community. It is only by liturgical action which fully dramatizes the formally social (the ministerial structure of the community and the particular ministry of particular sacramental actions) that the sense of the sacred is fully called forth. And it is only when the church experiences itself as a holy community that it can hear the scriptures as a word of love addressed to itself.

Having seen these principles at work in one liturgical gesture, the lighting of the new fire, it may be helpful to explore their possibilities (and their violations) in terms of other aspects of Catholic worship. The point of this next section is not to be exhaustive, but simply to illustrate further what I have already stated in principle.

The Liturgial Call to Primal Experience

Liturgical prayer always calls to some feature of primal experience. Our basic language and gestures of prayer rise out the very depth and center of our own personal history. Classic prayer postures involve the primal experience of the womb (kneeling with head bowed, or the profound prostration of Islam and some Eastern churches), or the crib (standing to greet the Lord, with hands upraised). There are anthropological, as well as theological reasons for the Madonna's having played such a significant role in Christian prayer through the centuries. The maternal character of the Madonna is an evocation of the sense of God as nurturing parent, as it is in terms of our own individual history, an evocation of our earliest experience as social beings. It is out of this experience of the interplay between mother and child that our sense of identity begins to emerge — and with it, our sense of community, for it is through knowing my place in relation to others that I experience myself as a member of a community. The sense of individuality and the sense of community are not opposites but complements: to the extent that we experience ourselves as cherished individuals do we experience ourselves as belonging to the community. In terms of ritual action, the primal sense of being cared for is evoked by a certain playfulness — the measured pace of gesture, the alternation of sound and silence, the doing of thoroughly non-utilitarian actions. To the extent that worship lacks these things, it will be experienced as a mere duty, to be gotten over as perfunctorily as possible. In terms of eucharistic celebration, the primal will be touched to the extent that our bodies are engaged in actions which reflect primal positions, and to the extent that our hearts are touched by the loving engagement in the playful action that is liturgy. If we lack a sense of community at worship, one of the most basic reasons is the virtual abandonment of gestures of community. Against the kneeling of the past, we have introduced mere standing with our hands at our sides or our eyes riveted in books — the very gestures of disengagement. We stand when we wait for buses, bored, in the same position which we now assume for major prayers and proclamations in the liturgy. We pray as we would when we want to avoid others, our eyes glued to a book (printed on newsprint, just like the uncommitted fellow commuter's newspaper).

The Liturgical Appeal to the Pre-social

Certain features of newer suburban churches bear an exact resemblance to fast food chain establishments. This is true not only in the abundance of plastic decoration (which might be acceptable: vulgarity will be an inevitable accompaniment of a truly popular liturgy), but also in the architectural arrangements. This is particularly true of our entrances: they are all designed for the easiest and quickest possible access between parking lot and pew. Whatever the disadvantages of older churches with their steep steps, at least coming to church was freighted with a sense of the importance of it all. The ordeal of getting up the steps told you that. This is not to press for the reintroduction of steep steps (not a good idea for the aged or the crippled, and a serious hazard for everyone in bad weather). But all serious social engagement involves not only the satisfactions of being and acting together, but also the ordeal of dealing with one another. Social interactions of any real significance are fraught with tension, whether it be the tension of eager anticipation or of dread. And if there is to be a genuine and authentic sense of community, then any serious assembly of the community will expose its members to that tension. Yet we build our churches wholly for convenience rather than for presenting entrants with the tension — and wonder why there is no sense of community when we are called to prayer. A good church entrance will eliminate anything that is physically dangerous, but it will heighten the sense that what is about to happen is both playful and communal. Some real space between parking lot and door is desirable, as is vestibule space where people can meet and greet one another, or where it can become at least evident that they are going to be expected to interact with one another.

This is why the ministry of ushers and (one hopes) the preparing of other ministers for eucharist (vesting, etc.) is best done in the vestibule through which all must pass. If some are uncomfortable with this, well enough. Membership in the Catholic Church is not always a comfortable thing.

The Liturgical Appeal to the Social

A good rite will enact the basic social structure of the

group, not only by what it says but also by what it does. As I have already suggested, the foundation of the experience of social structure lies at prior levels, the primal and the pre-social. It remains to be noted here that almost nothing in our present eucharistic pattern gives any play to a sense that the laity have a ministry to one another. This is why so many people experience the peace greeting as a shocking intrusion. It is the reason, too, for the weak quality of acclamation and response in our liturgical prayer. When everything in the environment militates against an experience of being together in a cooperative venture, verbal participation will indeed sink to a bare minimum. Both the architecture which is the environment of worship and the kinesthetic experience (the experience of touch, motion, and rest) serve in most cases to suggest emphatically that we have no relationship whatsoever to anyone other than the formally ordained or appointed ministers. The pew is a socially centripetal instrument of worship, serving to isolate individuals radically from one another. It is not the fixed character of pews, nor even their arrangement in rows which makes them so subversive of a sense of communion with one another. Public space demands fixed seating, for reasons of safety as well as durability. And the fixed seating of large numbers of people will demand some sort of seating in rows. But the present conventional arrangement is such that the sense of intercommunion with one another is utterly subverted. Visually, it is subverted by the paralleling of seating rows so that individual worshippers are unable to see any except those whose backs are to them, or who is facing them as a formal minister. A sense of bonding with other people requires a visual bonding whereby we can see something of other people's fronts or profiles. The pew is also kinesthetically sterile. Its very character as a bench causes us to draw in from one another, especially in our culture. Americans already have a bias toward withdrawing into anonymity in public places. We build our houses in the middle of lots, despite the fact that our front lawns are useless for anything other that the purely decorative. And with one of the world's best technologies, we have the world's most inefficient and chaotic public transportation because we prefer to be protected by the bubble of the individual auto. The pew serves that bias, and not only by separating us visually from others (just as the seats in airports do not make for conversation, but for isolation). The pew also causes us to draw in from one another because it puts us in peril of touching buttock to buttock if we get too close to one another. In a culture uncomfortable with physical contact of this sort, the result is paralyzing. People spontaneously put up emotive shields of protection against one another. The wearing of winter coats during services in heated churches is only symptomatic of an attitude encouraged by the surroundings. We are vigorously invited by the arrangement of the average parish church to keep totally to ourselves.

In such a setting, movement is experienced as happening alone, not something we do, but something I do, as processional movement is experienced only as my movement to and from the altar, and not as our gathering and dispersal from that central point.

Remedy is sometimes sought in gestures which further add to the tension: the "good morning" greeting of the presider to the congregation (the only person who says "good morning" to a group in expectation of a response is a schoolteacher), or the invitation to shake hands and introduce ourselves at the beginning of mass. The second is especially shocking, when the very architecture and movement patterns of the mass indicate that we are called upon to keep to ourselves.

In sum, nothing speaks directly to any real human sense of community except the words we use. And not surprisingly, the response is audibly feeble. To respond vigorously demands a sense of congruity between what is being said and what is happening. A liturgy whose choreography and architecture say that the laity are isolated individuals is incongrous when its texts and prayers say that the laity are an assembled community. This is why "catechesis" (understood as instruction of an informative sort) is insufficient for people to grasp and appreciate the spirit and forms of the liturgy. Effective catechesis can only be an interpretation of experience: that is what catechesis is about. If the basic experience of community is missing, no amount of instruction will make up for it.

The Liturgical Appeal to the Formally Social

As already indicated, the sense of the sacred arises fully when ordinary gestures are carried out dramatically in the context of prayer. If we have "lost the sense of mystery" it is because we have either trivialized gestures which were formerly robust and full, or we have failed to find ways which will not trivialize new gestures. There are four fundamental gestures which are the heart and center of Catholic sacramental worship: *assembling, bathing, dining, and embracing.* All our liturgical actions are elaborations of these fundamental human gestures.

Part of the power of our basic gestures is that they are rooted in primitive experience. Many higher mammals gather in flocks and herds. All of them clean themselves, eat, touch one another. Yet human beings add something of their own to these basic mammal functions. We do not merely gather, but we assemble. Not blind instinct, but a sense of history and common purpose brings us together. We not only wash, but also bathe. This is perhaps not as evident as a social event in daily American life as it is in certain other cultures, yet it is found in the familial bathing of babies and in our beachgoing habits. Likewise, not mere health but social necessity dictates our daily bathing habits. Bathing renews us, prepares us for a new day or a new event. I use the term *dining* advisedly. The eucharist is (inaccurately) frequently described as a "meal." I can best suggest the difference between dining and eating by observing that one prepares a dinner; one merely fixes a meal. A meal can be eaten alone, but it takes at least two for a dinner. The notion that people have difficulty appreciating the eucharist as dining because we do not dine every day is sheer non-sense. Dining is by definition "special"; we use it to mark special events: the barbecue or the festal table heaped high for family and friends, the dinner out for business and small social occasions, the banquet for the organization marking its hopes and its triumphs. Touching both comforts and empowers: it is the way we signal tenderness, as well as the way we single out people as especially powerful (note the crowds reaching for a president's touch — it is both a presidential acting out of his concern for the nation and a popular acknowledgement of his power).

Sacramental action, then, if it is to be genuinely effective as a communicator of the "sense of mystery," demands that these fundamental gestures be used carefully and dramatically. In certain significant ways, these gestures are vastly underplayed in our normal events of worship. Let us attend more closely to them one by one.

A. ASSEMBLING

We have already reflected on this matter at some length. The paschal vigil's lighting of the new fire is simply a highly elaborate assembling ritual, enhanced by the evocation of that most basic and loved human experience of gathering, the sharing of a common hearth and its light. Yet effective gathering rituals do not only speak of the warmth of sharing. Sharing is the result of ordeal. Peace with one another is hard-won, and a constant task. The paschal lighting of the new fire can function as an effective gathering ritual, precisely because it has the potential of presenting an ordeal (the discomfort of waiting in the dark, the breaking down of normal patterns of assembling). By contrast, our usual mode of entrance into eucharistic liturgy is bland and lack-luster, with no element of ordeal involved, and thus no relief of tension or sense of triumph that could bond us together. It is unfortunate in the extreme that we have had to abandon the eucharistic fast for all practical purposes. If we approach eucharistic celebration with the attitude of consumers, waiting only to "get something out of it," it is because we are asked to put so little into it. If we want more of a sense of celebration, we might well keep in mind that the difference between mere entertainment and real festivity is that true festivity requires a full commitment to spend freely. When people appear already sated, a feast is impossible. The event becomes a triviality or a redundancy, and is in any case boring because it costs so little.

But assembling requires not only a sense of passage through an ordeal. It also requires a sense of the social bonds we have with those present, the ritual evocation of the bonds we share with one another. As I have already suggested, there is virtually nothing in our present mode of entering a church and finding a seat that suggests real bonds between believers. This is the reason why our entrance rites are so incoherent and idiosyncratic, and rarely function as genuine invitations to the spirit of communal prayer so necessary to the hearing of the Word. The finding of appropriate signals of our bonds with one another is more complex, however, than the development of entrance rites. It is a matter which will be explored much further in subsequent chapters.

This is, however, the place to observe that the solution does not lie in the attempt to create a community of intimacy. It is too often assumed that "real community" is a community of intimacy, a community where people know one another well and care for one another as a family or as friends. Certain sorts of community are communities of intimacy — families are such communities, and so are certain kinds of religious community (though not all). Monika Hellwig has described the shape of Catholic community as a community of invitation: it invites all to a certain ideal, but it does not compel everyone to live up to it, as it tolerates considerable deviance from the ideal.[4] The fundamental bonds of Catholic community are not the bonds of intimacy, but are, rather, the bonds of faith, hope, and charity. We are not called together to be friends (though it may be

---

[4]See Monika Hellwig, *Tradition* (Dayton: Pflaum, 1974), 17-26.

very good if this happens). We are, rather, called together because we share a common ideal, a common commitment (however badly we may live them). What we come together to share is not necessarily intimacy, but our common values and our sense of a common share in them. This is why a Mass with a hundred thousand people in St. Peter's Square is so moving. It is not because people intimately know one another, but because they know that across the boundaries of place and language and origin, they share a common history of sin and grace, and a common hope.

We are perhaps too unreflective about the fact that public use of an intimate style normally reflects superficiality and a certain insincerity. The clerk who "honeys" us, the stranger on the elevator with a "hail fellow well met" attitude, the supercilious waiter, are generally experienced as obnoxious, and normally not taken too seriously. By way of contrast, beyond the circle of family and close friends, the deepest sorts of commitments may be expressed in an "impersonal" fashion. The fireman risking his life for a child may never see the child again, as the woman entrusting herself into the care of a surgeon knows nothing of his personal life. And Jesus' own most famous parable of the kind of love demanded of Christians speaks not of an intimate encounter, but of a stranger's meeting the need of another stranger and going on his way.

If we are truly to come to grips with the matter of assembling, i.e. if we are really to develop some real sense of being a community responsive and responsible to one another, attention needs to be paid to the ways we signal that responsiveness and that responsibility in ritual. For the moment, our experience of that is virtually nil.

B. BATHING

There are a number of features inherent in any experience of an act of bathing; they are its irreducible core. One of them is that it involves the taking of time. Bathing, to be done well, requires a leisurely pace. It is mere washing if it is rushed. Bathing is also not a tidy enterprise. People get wet and put in disarray, and the surroundings do also. Because of the messiness of the task, and because of our own vulnerability, either because of our own nakedness or because we are never fully in control of the baby we are bathing, there is also an inherently embarrassing side to bathing. In the tub or at the beach, we are something less than our most noble and elegant selves. Perhaps no liturgical symbol has become more robbed of its power than that of the baptismal water, precisely because we seek to obliterate those features which are most evocative to a real event of bathing. We are reluctant to take the time, whether it be to baptize adults at the Easter vigil, or children at Sunday eucharist. We are horrified if anything is messy and out of place, and the conventional baptism is as antiseptic as intravenous feeding. We are horrified by the thought of even the nakedness of infants in church, or worse, for that matter, by the thought of mussing milady's coiffure. Baptism, according to St. Paul, is a burial into Christ's death. This might come home with some vividness if we recovered the courage to let people and the baptistry get really wet, if shame and discomfort were accepted as normal parts of this special kind of ritual, and if we were willing to experience this sacrament for what it is, less a piece of festivity (this belongs more to Confirmation) and more a piece of work that flashes out in ritual the kind of struggle that Christian life is going to be. Baptisms at Sunday eucharist are rare because it would be "inconvenient" for people, and "uncomfortable." No doubt. So is birth inconvenient and uncomfortable, and not only for the one being born.

C. DINING

In certain significant ways, the present rite of Mass is able to be experienced as an event of dining, at least in the sense that the interplay between priest and assembly is, at its best, able to be experienced as a dramatic interplay between a host and his guests. But the weakness in our rites of gathering spills over into eucharistic celebrating, and so it is still experienced less as a celebration together than an encounter between priest and a collection of individual people, with a weak sense of ties to one another. Some of this could be alleviated by a more serious use of lay ministry in the liturgy — and by serious I mean by letting them appear clearly as lay people. If lay ministers (reader, prayer leader for the Prayer of the Faithful, special communion ministers) came forward from the congregation to exercise their ministries rather than being seated in the sanctuary like unfrocked clergy, there would be a sense of flow between altar and pew which would suggest ritually that we have the responsibility of care for one another in the liturgy. With present seating arrangements, lay ministers can only be experienced as delegates of the priest — thus perpetuating the sense that the liturgy is a clerical event that happens only "up there" at the altar.

One of the features of present conventional celebration is its generally didactic tone (The theme of today's mass is . . . this gospel means . . .). It is doubtless the kind of didacticism that has invaded our worship which permits the manners of the schoolroom — the oddity of greeting people with "Good morning," and the peculiarity of reciting psalms and hymns (e.g. the Glory to God). We have come to view the Liturgy of the Word as primarily instructional, a view that is clearly manifest in our choice of a lectern, a distinctively school-roomish instrument, upon which to enthrone the sacred writings. Such didacticism militates against the sense of dining. The kind of speech appropriate to dining is that of storytelling, of the sharing of the common history of the group. If there are strangers present, an effort will be made to forge a common history out of the sharing of separate stories. But this does not have information as its primary function. Its primary function is to enhance a sense of bonds within the community that shares the dinner. The kind of information that pertains to learning about the community's ways of rule-keeping or housekeeping is kept to a minimum, and mostly reserved to other occasions. If one is such a stranger, that one cannot share the group's jokes and legends, one is expected to enquire further, outside the event of dining. If the Liturgy of the Word could be experienced more as a telling of the community's common story, and less as an event of informing people for the first time what the basic elements of the story are, it would doubtless create a deeper sense of sharing in eucharistic celebrations.[5]

D. TOUCHING

In contrast to bathing, which is fraught with a sense of incompleteness and passage, touching gestures are essentially affirmative, speaking of fullness and completion, of tension resolved and of common unity achieved. Through touching them, the church marks out people's place and status in the assembly. The anointing of baptism and confirmation mark us as full members, as the hand-laying of ordination sets people apart for special and public service in the church. Doubtless, the truncation of these gestures into dabbings with minuscule amounts of oil, or the most perfunctory sort of hand-laying, robs them of any evocative power. If people lack a sense of place in the eucharistic liturgy, it surely has much to do with the fact that we fall short of fully ritualizing the belief that they *should* have a place.

And so we have suggested in this chapter that the experience of eucharist has everything to do with our experience of other sacraments as well, particularly of baptism and confirmation. In the next chapter, we will indicate more

---

[5]One of the major concerns of real liturgical renewal would be the rediscovery of the scriptures as our own story. Liturgical prayer, rooted and grounded as it is in scripture, demands that people be able to see themselves as participants in the biblical story. This is not a matter of learning "Bible history," but of developing a spirituality grounded in scripture — one of the major tasks of a real catechumenate. It is not a matter, however, of developing such a spirituality simply for catechumens (those preparing for baptism), but of recovering this spirituality for the already baptized as well. This is a task which cannot be accomplished simply within the context of Sunday preaching — the lectionary readings are developed on the presupposition that the congregation (at least in significant numbers) *already* sees itself in the light of the biblical story. Significant efforts to do this for the already baptized have already begun. See James Dunning, "The Rite of Christian Initiation of Adults: Model of Adult Growth," *Worship* 53 (1979), 142-156.

clearly why these three sacraments are integrally related to one another.

Recommended Reading

Gallen, John, "The Necessity of Ritual," *The Way* 13 (1973) 270-282.

Erikson, Erik, *Toys and Reasons, Stages in the Ritualization of Experience* (New York: W.W. Norton and Co., 1977).

Lawler, M., "Christian Rituals: An Essay in Sacramental Symbolism," *Horizons* 7 (Spring, 1980) 7-35.

Mitchell, Leonel, *The Meaning of Ritual*, (New York: Paulist Press, 1977).

Nouwen, Henri, *The Living Reminder* (New York: Seabury, 1977).

CHAPTER VII

THE FULLNESS OF EUCHARISTIC COMMUNION
The Eucharist as Sacrament of Initiation

As suggested in the last chapter, most of our sacramental experience is vicarious and retrospective. What is important about our sacramental experience is not simply what happens to us in the moment or on the day of "reception," but rather, our appreciation of the sacraments is conditioned by our ongoing experience of the way they are celebrated. We do not appreciate baptism simply by being baptized, but we appreciate it, plumb its depths by the repeated experience of the baptism of *others*. It is the cumulative experience of sacraments which impresses us with their meaning.

There is also, or at least can be, a certain "ecology" of sacraments as well, as suggested in Chapters V and VI. This is especially true of the relationship between baptism and confirmation on the one hand, and eucharist on the other. Originally, the eucharist was experienced as the finale of Christian initiation: full participation in the eucharist marked the emergence of the newly baptized as full-fledged and responsible members of the Christian community. The doing of eucharist represents a celebration of the grace and commitment of our baptism.

Unfortunately, that intimate connection between bap-

tism and confirmation and the eucharist as the sacrament of
mature Christian commitment has been badly obscured
over the ages, and in many ways still remains obscured. I
would go so far as to suggest that this is our single most
important problem with eucharistic celebration. If eucharistic celebration is lackluster, sporadic, weak, "boring," a
"distraction", the problem is not ultimately one of ceremony
or celebrants.[1] And it is not a problem which can be solved
by individual worshippers, it is beyond the control of individuals. It lies in the failure to appreciate[2] the eucharist as
the offering of all the baptized. And if we are to recover a
deeper and richer and fuller sense of what it means for the
baptized to offer the eucharist, we need a full review of our
present baptismal (and confirmational) practice. The "ecology" of sacraments is such that the way we do and appreciate one sacrament will affect our practice and
understanding of another. We cannot have eucharistic renewal without baptism renewal as well.[3]

It is axiomatic in sacramental theology that sacraments
are signs and they are actions of the church. What a sacramental action does, most immediately and obviously and
concretely, is to enact a model of the church, to reflect in
action what the church understands to be its mission in the
world. By implication, and by indirection, the sacramental
action will speak for other realities too — it implies a certain
understanding of Christ (Christology) and a certain under-

---

[1]The frequent statement, "Well, after all, it is really up to the priest," is only a
diagnosis of our present liturgical situation. The design of the new liturgy is that a
variety of ministries be operative, and to the extent that "it all depends on the
priest," to that extent we have failed to achieve a reformed and renewed liturgy. See
my "Liturgical Ministry," *Emmanuel* 84 (1978) 511-515; also Aidan Kavanagh,
"Ministries in the Community and in the Liturgy," in Schmidt, M. (ed.),
Liturgy: Self-Expression of the Church (Concilium 72) 55-67.

[2]By "appreciate," I do not refer simply to a matter of attitude or feeling. I mean
the active prizing, cherishing, and valuing initiation in the actual practice of the
church. Clearly, for instance, we appreciate ordination, requiring all sorts of
preparation, and being careful to solemnize it with public ceremony. We are
infinitely more casual about baptism.

[3]See Aidan Kavanagh, *The Shape of Baptism* (New York: Pueblo, 1978),
especially 158-163.

standing of the Spirit (pneumatology), as it inevitably implies a certain understanding of God (theology), and a certain view of the world (cosmology) — items we explored in the opening chapters of this book. But it only speaks for these things — God, Christ, Spirit, world — through the medium of its enacting a model of the church.[4] The consequence of the axiom that sacraments are sign-actions of the church is that sacramental action will make an immediate statement about the church, its mission, and its ministry: all other statements are mediated through the enactment of the set of relationships which constitute church. Translated into a contemporary idiom, this means that the sacraments are the language through which the community of faith identifies itself. In sacramental action, the church both discovers and expresses its self-understanding.

This language of faith will find full and supreme expression in eucharistic action. The operative model of church will be expressed above all in the shape of the church's eucharist. This is evident if we compare the very different models of the church embodied in the medieval rite of Mass on one hand, and in contemporary eucharistic celebration on the other. In the medieval Mass, the prevailing model of church as institution was dramatically signaled in every detail of the rite, from the exalting of the role of the clergy as over against the more passive and minimal role of the laity (significantly, the laity came to be represented at the altar by *child* ministers) to such details as the legalese of the language introducing the institution narrative in the Canon.[5] The scrupulous attention to detail in the rite (legalism) was not something really extraneous to it. The conceiving of the church as institution, and the living out of that model, demanded a rite which would speak in every way for the church's self-understanding, and that self-understanding

[4] For a full exploration of the idea of model, see Avery Dulles, *Models of the Church* (Garden City: Doubleday, 1974).

[5] Our present translation modifies (rightly) the very legal language of the Latin original, which prays that the sacrifice may be "right, reasonable, approved, and acceptable" before citing the story of the last supper.

was itself juridical. The role of ministry is critical in an ecclesial rite. The medieval Mass, the role of the priest as mediator, whether of grace or of tradition, was exalted, while the role of the laity was minimized.[6] This spoke for a church in which the hierarchy were seen as the bearers of mission while the laity were conceived as simple passive recipients of ministry. Everything from architecture to language heightened the sense of distance between clergy and laity.

Today's rite, however, with the priest facing the people and speaking their own language, flanked by other adult lay ministers, projects a very different model of the church. The model is much more familial: the values of dialogue and sharing come to the fore. Whatever the exact relationship between rite and life may be, the contemporary liturgical statement is matched by a rising desire for more inclusive patterns of church life.

As I have already suggested, the kind of Christological statement that a liturgical action makes will hinge upon its ecclesial statement. If "Christology from above," a Christology which concentrated mainly on what separates Christ from us prevailed through most of our history, it had everything to do with a liturgical praxis which exalted the distance between clergy and laity, as it separated laity from the altar. The medieval liturgy was filled with symbols of separation, from architecture which divided nave and sanctuary, to ornaments which sharply distinguished ministers from people, to rubrics which heightened the sense of the liturgical action's being apart from the ordinary. By enacting ecclesial separations, the church projected a Christology which marked out Christ as the unique One. By way of contrast, today's liturgical celebration, exalting the familial

---

[6]For a study of the progressive mutation of the role of the priest from representative of the community to representative of the (institutional) church, see Edward Schillebeeckx, "The Christian Community and its Office-Bearers" in *The Right of the Community to a Priest (Concilium* 133, 1980), 95-134. This development in many ways coincides with the progressive exaltation of the priestly role in the liturgy.

and the communal, lends itself to more of a "Christology from below," which stresses the points of contact and unity between Christ and ourselves.

Finally, we can observe that the implied Christological statement leads to a cosmological one, and thus to a statement about the relationship between God and the world. A "Christology from above" tends to a very negative judgement upon the world which lies beyond the immediate ambit of the church — a tendency that is already found in the Johannine writings. With the sense of Christ's distance from people and the world, there is a corresponding heightening of the sense of the world as lost, dark, sinful. In the medieval Roman rite, especially in its eucharistic liturgy, that sense is manifest in its preoccupation with sin. Entrance, offertory, and communion rite all came to be developed as penitential gestures, as the classic Canon with its medieval rubrics appeared as an act of impetration for the forgiveness of sins. The relationship between God and the world was articulated primarily in terms of an issue of guilt — a religious perception which pervaded everything in the old Roman rite from the paschal *Exsultet* to the blessing of objects with holy water.

By way of contrast, despite certain failures in the reform of preparatory rites,[7] the current Roman eucharistic liturgy embodies a brighter and broader Christology. Doubtless, the popularity of the offertory *berakoth* ("Blessed are you . . ." etc.) recited over the bread and cup, generally recited aloud against the rubrical preference for silence, constitutes a witness to a more positive estimate of the relationship between Christ, church and world. To speak of bread and wine as the products both of nature and of human skill and striving, and to identify such as potential food and drink for life everlasting is to pray in a very different fashion than the very penitential prayers of the medieval offertory rite. The

----

[7]See my articles, "Our Cluttered Vestibule: The Unreformed Entrance Rite," *Worship* 48 (1974) 270-277; and "Preparation of the Altar and Gifts or Offertory," *Worship* 48 (1974) 595-600.

Christology of these new thanksgivings is allied to the understanding of the Spirit of the Eucharistic Prayer III, which identifies the Spirit as working first in the whole of creation, then in history and the church, finally in this assembly, and at last, upon this altar.[8] The Spirit is portrayed not as coming as from above, but in a concentric movement which embraces the whole of creation.

The projection of the model of church in eucharistic celebration will normally be matched with the model of church sustained by initiatory patterns. That is to say, initiatory patterns will enact the same model of church as eucharistic celebration does. Thus, the church of the late second and early third century, which celebrated the eucharist as an oblation of the whole church, found the climax of initiation in the admission to the eucharistic table of the newly baptized as robed and anointed priests, prophets, and kings. Likewise, the institutional model of church which came to prevail in the medieval West was thoroughly acted out in initiatory practice. If baptism became more and more privatized, if first confession came to constitute the first conscious moment of initiation, and if in the end, confirmation came to be celebrated after first communion, this was all entirely consistent with the institutional model of church. If the laity are primarily the passive subjects of the clergy's ministry, if religion is mainly a matter of dealing with guilt, and if indeed the Spirit of God is bound to ecclesiastical institutions, there is no better way of signing that sort of conception of church than the initiatory patterns which actually developed and came to prevail.

Sacraments, we say, effect what they signify; and they do it, we claim, *ex opere operato*. What I have attempted to suggest is that it really does not require much faith to assent

---

[8]See the portion of the prayer between the *Holy* and the institution narrative (consecration). Affirming that all life and holiness find their source in God by the work of the Spirit, the prayer goes on to praise God for gathering a people from age to age and from east to west so that a perfect offering may glorify God. The prayer goes on, "And so, Father, we bring you these gifts," praying that the Spirit will be operative so as to make them the body and blood of Christ.

to these notions, properly understood. Such classic asser-
tions are reflective of simple facts of life and of the nature of
ritual — that the impact of ritual action will be to present a
model of the way the church lives and understands itself.
And so, if religion is seen mainly as a matter of dealing with
guilt, and the church as institution is perceived as the proper
agent to deal with it, then there is indeed everything to be
said for the first confession's constituting the first conscious
initiatory event. The initiate's experience will be entirely
consonant with the church's self-understanding. Likewise, if
in the final analysis what constitutes the proper Christian
life is adherence to the teaching of the hierarchy and obedience to its commands, and if sacramental grace is circum-
scribed by its reception at the hands of the clergy, then there
could be no more fitting closure to Christian initiation than
episcopal confirmation, preferably at an age when one fully
understands what one is doing.

In the light of the above observations, the present initiatory problem is that we have retained a pattern of initiation
dictated by the institutional model of church while at the
same time beginning to project a very different model of
church in both ordinary eucharistic and baptismal celebration. We use ceremonies which speak for a communal and
participatory model of church, while retaining a pattern
which speaks for the institutional model. This is confusion
by definition, and it is ritualism by definition. And this is to
pay attention only to tactics while ignoring strategy.

Whatever may be the place of "preparation" programs of
one sort or another, and whatever may be the utility of
administering certain sacraments at certain ages, we need to
notice that the real question is not one of the age of either
first confession or of confirmation (the conventional way of
posing the issue). The real question is what our initiatory
pattern *as a whole* tends to say. Then, the critical events
(whatever they may be concretely) are: *the onset of initiation, the first conscious experience of initiation, and the
sacramental finale of initiation.* These will have everything
to do with what both the individual subject and the church

as a whole will come to understand as the meaning of initiation. This is precisely what has been delineated above, in terms of what the initiatory continuum meant within the institutional model of the medieval and post-Tridentine church. If we are going to be faithful to the model of the church projected not only in our current eucharistic rite, but also in the rites for the baptism not only of adults but those for children as well, the continuing of first confession before first communion and the separation of confirmation from first eucharist both pose serious problems. For the model of the church projected in the rites of both baptism and eucharist is robustly communal and vigorously participatory.[9] There is no denial that the ordinary believer is a sinner subject to the ministrations of the clergy. But the point is, these are not the aspects of the church which prevail to constitute a model. These are things which enter into the definition of a believing Christian, but they do not exhaust nor even begin definitively to constitute what it means to be a believing Christian. What actually prevails in the new rites in the constitution of the believer is that the individual is seen as a responsive and responsible member of an assembly of co-believers. Ministry is not limited to the ministry of the ordained, and mission is the task of the whole church. Even in the case of the baptism of children, who are not yet capable of response, considerable stress is laid on the community's (not just the parents') responsibility to call the children to that response. The model of the believer is eucharistic, not penitential.

If the model of the church as cooperative, communal, and participatory and sharing in a common mission is to be signed out adequately in sacramental celebration, it goes without saying that the preference for the baptism of children at the Sunday eucharist needs to be asserted as a practical norm. Despite certain inadequacies,[10] the rite does

[9]This was already fully affirmed in the Constitution on the Liturgy; see especially Chapters I and II.

[10]The three stages, welcome by the church, preparatory rites (word/prayer/exorcism) and actual baptism, might well be solemnized at separate times, over a

constitute a call to the community to a sense of its own baptismal awareness. I would go so far as to suggest that parishes which lay their stress on the preparation of *parents* for the baptism of children have entirely missed the point of the new rite. The distinctively new features of the rite are not on the responsibilities of parents (these are clearly found in the Catechism of the Council of Trent), but in what it has to say about the *responsibilities of the believing community, and what it demands that they affirm publicly.* The desperate need is for the preparation of *congregations* for the baptism of children in their midst. As anyone knows who deals seriously with adult formation, it is notoriously difficult to assess "commitment" except in certain limited situations, as it is notoriously difficult to know what actually calls forth conversion and commitment. We have already noted Monika Hellwig's suggestion that one of the distinctive characteristics of Roman Catholicism is precisely that it is not a community of the converted — that as a policy it invites commitment without compelling it.[11] This should be a cue for the treatment of adults. Let us, by all means, have a pastoral outreach to the parents of newborns. But let us not make it one more ritual hoop whose reward is a sacrament. In our present context, we might well become more aware of the parabolic character of sacramental celebration — that it often speaks less for a reality achieved than for a hope expressed, that it presents a challenge and an invitation to something not fully realized, that sacramental action reveals not who we are, but who we may be. We could do no better than to begin with the discomfort most people feel with Sunday baptism at eucharist, and reflect upon the experience, taking it as a starting point for suggesting that the church is speaking for values other than speed, convenience, cheap grace and easy affirmation, and that has much to do with responsibility for one another. Young parents

period of time. The present rite easily becomes drearily didactic ("preachy"), as the compression of its rich symbols into one act tends to diminish the power of any of them.

[11]See Chapter VI, p. 110.

need to be the subject of the church's care, not its condemnation and suspicion. The people who need to be challenged at the time of childbirth are not the young parents, but the indifferent others.

If we really do take the church seriously as being cooperative, communal, participatory, and as endowed with a sense of common mission in the world, we need to take first eucharist much more seriously than we do. Its privatization into domestic or small group celebration is *not* to take it seriously: like the baptism of infants, the first eucharist of children should constitute a call to the assembly to ponder the import of standing to share in the eucharist. Since we rely on a rather debased conventional view of first eucharist, we tend to think of it as the first *reception* of communion. Yet if the General Instruction on the Order of Mass is to be taken seriously, what comes to the fore is that the assembly is not seen primarily as a gathering of receivers, but as an assembly of co-offerers.[12] Virtually every change in the rite of Mass since Vatican II has been directed to the service of that end,[13] as the General Instruction describes the eucharistic prayer as the high point of the entire celebration, precisely because it is to be understood as expressing the offering of the whole church.[14] From the point of view of the Sacramentary, as of pre-medieval Catholicism, participation in eucharist is the expression of the Christian commitment *par excellence*. From this perspective, there is indeed a certain appropriateness to deferring first eucharist until there can be some conscious appreciation of what is taking place. At about the onset of school age, children begin to experience themselves as responsible agents in the world.

There is, then, a real inappropriateness to placing the kind of stress that we often do on confirmation as a sacra-

---

[12]See especially Chapter I, or the important statement about the eucharistic prayer in Chapter II, "The meaning of the Prayer is that the *whole assembly* offers the sacrifice." (#54).

[13]See the general directives to that purpose in Chapters II and III in the Constitution on the Liturgy.

[14]General Instruction, #54.

ment having to do with a "mature" Christian commitment. It is only derivatively, and in relation to its being a sealing of baptism or an anointing for eucharistic participation that it can be understood as a sacrament having to do with commitment. Significantly, in the rite of confirmation for those baptized in infancy, the only way the Christian commitment can be ritually evoked is by the renewal of baptismal promises on the one hand and by sharing in the eucharist on the other. It should be noted, too, that according to our present rites, it is not confirmation but the eucharist which has to do with the imparting of the Spirit for what might be called "maturity." Both Eucharistic Prayer III and Eucharistic Prayer IV portray the eucharistic action as a work of the Spirit, as they portray the purpose of the eucharist as imparting the Spirit sacramentally for the building up of the church.[15] If there is an "ongoing" sacramental gift of the Spirit, it is to be found in eucharistic participation. In view of Roman Catholic preoccupations with transubstantiation, it is especially noteworthy that the eucharistic body of Christ upon the altar is seen "instrumentally," as subordinated to the work of the Spirit for the building up of the church.

There is a certain bias that there are "pastoral" reasons for confirming apart from either baptism or first eucharist (its association with either one would find ready justification). If that means that there is a need for some kind of pastoral care of adolescents, including catechesis on sacraments, fine. We do need *something* that says loudly and clearly that we care about adolescents. In a church governed by bishops such as our own, people have a right to see a bishop in their parish some time before they reach adulthood. But we could have the pastoral care of adolescents and episcopal visitation without confirmation. It might even make a very powerful statement about eucharist if we insisted that first

---

[15]Significantly, after the consecration, the eucharistic prayer asks that those who share in the eucharist will be filled with the *Holy Spirit*. Christ's eucharistic presence under the forms of bread and wine is not an end in itself, but for the purpose of imparting the life of the Spirit.

eucharists be presided over by the bishop. But for the rest, it is more and more difficult to understand what sense adolescent confirmation makes. Even if confirmation were primarily about affirming adult commitment, the obvious thing about adolescents is that they are not ready for it. Adolescence is by very definition a condition of being non-involved in the adult world. Outside of the cultures which initiate to adulthood in puberty (and the initiate emerges a fully enfranchised adult), a ritual moment of "adult" commitment makes no sense whatever.

Finally, since in the Roman rite, confirmation has an undeniably pneumatic (Spirit-oriented) character, there is something extremely dangerous about its removal from the initiatory continuum. Western Christianity has been notorious for its extremes — on the one side, a fissiparous sectarianism, and on the other, hierarchical authoritarianism. It has likewise been bedeviled by a certain individualistic spirit and by a pervasive legalism. We may well ask questions about the precedence of ritual chicken over societal egg. But in any case, historically our rites of initiation have found their finale, not in the welcome of the baptized to the common table of the faithful, but in the individual's kneeling before the bishop to receive the Spirit. This suggests that rite and culture may have more to do with one another than we would like to think. The problem is that when the invocation of the Spirit is allowed to dangle free from the ordinary life of the church, the Spirit will be sought everywhere except within that common life.

Against this backdrop, it should be obvious that our present initiatory continuum is not only a theological problem, but also a pastoral anomaly. As I have attempted to suggest, at least in indirect ways, the retention of the first confession of children before their first communion is not simply a violation of what contemporary psychology knows of the development of conscience. It also constitutes a contribution to the general confusion as to what sacraments are for and what the church is about. Given the model of the church projected in the Sacramentary and in our baptismal rites both for adults and for children, the kind of sacramental statement made by first confession of children before first communion is one that is both pastorally inept and theologically indefensible. Having already suggested why our present confirmation praxis is both pastorally and theologically indefensible, I can only add one more observation. It is psychologically indefensible as well. Studies of religious development more and more indicate that conversion is a continual process. Sacramental celebration needs to be seen not as expressing conversion fully accomplished, but simply as providing a language for it. The learning of a language, even a ritual language, belongs to the onset of a process, not to its term. It is no more inappropriate to confirm in early childhood than it is to baptize and to permit first eucharist. Moreover, if conversion is to be understood as an ongoing process, there is everything to be said for the sacramental conclusion of initiation in eucharist, the one initiatory sacrament which is repeatable for a lifetime.

Those who work with sacramental preparation programs are often deeply concerned about people's sense of Christian community and their sense of commitment. It has been suggested to me that we Catholics do not really, in the final analysis, lack either community or commitment, but that instead we are a community of reticence. I am inclined to agree. Close attention to the faith of the inarticulate suggests that what we really lack is not so much either commitment or community as we lack the facility to express it to one another. Anyone who works with adults in any way that comes near their real spiritual concerns and their real spiritual development becomes aware, not of a lack of faith, but of a lack of language to express faith. All too often, the journey of conversion is experienced as something quite other than what people assume the church is about. This disparity is, no doubt, due to the disparity between our present initiatory situation and what people actually experience. For it is part of the adult journey of conversion to experience oneself becoming a responsive and responsible adult in faith. As long as our initiatory language (i.e. the language of rite, not simply the language of speech) remains tied to an obsolete model of faith and the church, that dichotomy between experience and ritual will remain, and with it, the vacuous sense of loss and longing that now so often attends Catholic life.

Language is not simply the property of individuals. It is common property, or it is not language. That is why feminists can object to sexist language, even when it is not personally "meant" by the user as oppressive. The very structures of language are communal, and therefore what we say has communal effect and participates in common meanings. This is as true of the language of ritual as it is of the language of simple speech. And because the language of ritual is a communal language, it is by the living of the rhythms of the community that one plumbs its meaning — by using it over and over again. If we have a problem with adult "commitment" in the Catholic church, it is because we so radically obscure its language. If the experience of conversion has become separated from the language of conversion, it is because the term of conversion is not clearly expressed in the term of initiation. That is to say, our present initiatory patterns make it less than obvious that the whole point of being baptized is to stand with one's co-believers as a responsible bearer of the church's mission to be the body of Christ dead and risen in the world. The real initiatory question, while it may indeed involve both first confession and confirmation, and demand a thoroughgoing critique of both, actually has to do directly with neither sacrament. It has to do with the fact that present practice radically obscures the character of the eucharist as standing with baptism as a premier sacrament of initiation. If confusion and resentment attend current praxis, well they may. Our liturgies are ceremonially and tactically familial and participatory, while structurally and strategically (in relationship to one another) they are institutional. Our liturgical praxis of initiation sounds an uncertain trumpet indeed.

If Catholic worship has come to lack a sense of mystery and of the sacred, if there is a sense of incoherence and lack of direction, if it seems not to connect adequately with ordinary life, if it is experienced as neither sanctifying the world in which we live nor arousing us to action to change that world, much of this tragic failure lies in the inevitable confusion that occurs when liturgical tactics are in conflict with liturgical strategy. As it has been the burden of this book to suggest, Roman Catholic liturgical reform was not aimed at destroying the sense of the sacred, but at relocating it, not as being somewhere "out there," but as being in the midst of the assembly. We will not fully grasp this, i.e.share in this perception with a "full and active participation of mind and body" until our initiatory strategy aims at actively cherishing the role of the individual in the midst of the assembly. When private Sunday afternoon baptisms and rectory weddings become as unthinkable as ordination in a sacristy, we will have people coming to the eucharist with a sense of the weight of what they are doing.

Recommended Reading

Kavanagh, Aidan, *The Shape of Baptism* (New York: Pueblo, 1978).

Gallen, John, ed., *Made, Not Born* (Notre Dame: University of Notre Dame Press, 1976).

Searle, Mark, *Christening* (Leigh-on-Sea, Essex: Kevin Mayhew, 1977).

CHAPTER VIII

TO PRAY THE EUCHARIST
The Problem of Piety in Contemporary Religious Consciousness

Until a generation ago, most eucharistic piety, in fact most piety generally, centered around the worship of the eucharistic host and around Christ's sacrifice understood as an atonement for sin in the medieval sense of a ransom paid to God. Even prayer to Mary, for instance, was preoccupied with that view of ourselves as sinners — it is reflected in such staples as the Hail Mary, the *Salve Regina*, and the *Memorare*. For reasons that I have indicated already in Chapter III, the whole idea of atonement sacrifice has become problematic for contemporary piety, and cannot grip the hearts of people as it once did. There are also problems with centering piety around the worship of Christ present under the forms of bread and wine. This can be such a sensitive issue that I must hasten now before going on to note that for the first thousand years of the Catholic Church's history, it did not occur to people to make the consecrated elements the objects of worship! They were treated as holy things to be used reverently, but it did not occur to people to center prayers on them.

For reasons which I will now explore, it is increasingly difficult for people to relate to worship of the host. As I have already indicated, this has nothing to do with belief in

Christ's real presence under the forms of bread and wine. That belief does not necessarily impel worship (it in fact did not for a thousand years), much less inspire a piety. For the worship of the host depended upon a whole world of suppositions and assumptions which have begun to drop away as it was supported by the ceremonial of the Mass rite itself. The worship of the host has everything to do with the general experience of God as an invader from outside our world. Piety concentrated on the moment when Christ came to be present under the form of bread and wine, lingering over that aspect of the eucharistic liturgy which projected a view of divine presence coming from outside to within the world. This was supported by the very masculine gesture of elevation, which required hand-eye coordination, the very starting point of technology. In a liturgy where Christ is understood as present first of all within the world and the assembly, and present on the altar because of that presence first in the church, the event of consecration is simply an unfolding of that presence from within, and is less dramatically marked. This is precisely what we find in our new eucharistic rite. This is true above all of Eucharistic Prayer III (a Sunday favorite in this country) which speaks of the work of the Spirit in the world and in the church and then moves on to ask for the coming of the Spirit to consecrate the bread and wine:

> Father, you are holy indeed,
> and all creation rightly gives you praise,
> All life, all holiness comes from you
> through your Son, Jesus Christ our Lord,
> by the working of the Holy Spirit.
> From age to age you gather a people to yourself,
> so that from east to west
> a perfect offering may be made
> to the glory of your name.
>
> And so, Father, we bring you these gifts,
> We ask you to make them holy by the power of

your Spirit,
that they may become the body and blood
of your Son, our Lord Jesus Christ,
at whose command we celebrate this eucharist.

The high drama of the new eucharistic rite comes, less at the elevation of the host and chalice at the consecration, which is very modest, than at the doxology, where, identifying ourselves with Christ ("through Him, with Him, in Him, in the unity of the Holy Spirit"), we present ourselves united to Christ to the Father. This speaks eloquently for a Christ within the community, and for a eucharistic celebration that speaks, not for a God who intervenes from without, but who is present with his people in all their time of sorrow and joy.

In view of this, to the extent that people enter into a contemporary religious consciousness, former practices such as Benediction may not only be obsolete but also profoundly alienating if they are promoted for a people who have ceased to need them.

At the same time, the passage from older pieties to new is often very difficult. Even when particular styles of prayer have lost their utility, the loss is not always easy. Frequently, people assume that because they can no longer pray in ways that they used to pray, that they do not or cannot pray at all. This is such a common problem that it requires some serious reflection here.

And the problem goes far beyond the question of liturgical prayer. Far more than we realize, there is always a real relationship between liturgical prayer, popular piety, and spirituality. As long as the liturgy projected an image of God as "out there," as the holy other who enters the world from without, it was natural to pray as if God could be addressed exactly like another human person "out there" in front of us. If we are to develop an authentic contemporary eucharistic piety, then the whole question of piety today must be addressed. Here, then, I will explore some basic questions of styles of prayer, not only in a eucharistic context, but also outside it.

For many people, one of the most disconcerting features of the Christian spiritual life has become the convention of speaking of God, Jesus Christ, or the Holy Spirit primarily as though they were persons who are somehow to be intimately known as lover, companion, friend, or parent. Sometimes, the uncritical and reflective use of this sort of language can be one of the most significant barriers to growth in the life of the Spirit. There are many people who assume that they either do not or cannot pray authentically because they do not find themselves experiencing a "personal" presence of God, i.e., a sense of a divine Other present as friend, lover, companion, or parent. Since they so view themselves as flawed believers, such people are, at the very least, deprived of something of the joy and freedom of the children of God. Where this felt lack is also accompanied by a seriousness about the things of the Spirit, the result can verge on torment. In a situation where someone seeks spiritual guidance, the client behaves in a manner similar to the way sexual deviance is often revealed. The client talks all around the subject, presents literature which touches the issue obliquely or in principle but not directly, throws out hints, and wilts with relief when the awful truth is finally out and the guide passes no judgement.

All too often, however, the matter is never dealt with adequately through spiritual advice and guidance, and relief is sought in a vain quest for signs and wonders, a search for something that will offset the sense of divine disfavor. It is perhaps one of the major sources of the alienated religiosity, which not being personally secure, seeks validation in convincing others. Often enough, too, the spiritual disquiet over an assumed flaw of this sort will find an outlet wherever the personality is weakest. Sexual disorder, for instance, may be dramatically aggravated by this sort of anguish.

The conventional Christian "personalism" is also at times a major deterent to the embracing of the Christian faith. People undergoing religious and spiritual conversion, yet not in any way experiencing what they could identify as a "personal" presence, assume that whatever else might be involved, it could not be the God of the Christian faith.

In the experience of this writer, at least, this problem of Christian "personalism" is *not* a problem for the naive, the simple, or the theologically uneducated. Intuitively and unreflectively, they seem to be able to deal with various languages of piety with the appropriate accuracy and the right sort of tentativeness. This is why the worst sort of fundamentalist jargon or devotionalistic saccharine can sound wholly authentic on the lips of some people. They seem to possess a certain untroubled "savvy" about when such language is appropriate and when it is not. On the other hand, I have found that it is the brighter sort of seminarian, or the university graduate, who can be utterly thrown by the assumption that a serious person of faith and prayer should experience God literally as lover, companion, friend, or parent.

This may be in some ways a new problem for Roman Catholicism. We have perhaps forgotten how relatively rare direct address to God actually was in the preconciliar experience of the practices of piety. He was either addressed through the medium of rite, or through the imaginative medium of the intercession of the saints. Even address to Jesus Christ was a mediated address — either through Jesus Christ present in the Blessed Sacrament or through some *aspect* of Jesus Christ — to Christ Crucified, or the Sacred Heart, for instance. Roman Catholics did not simply and nakedly address the Lord Jesus Christ, much less God the Father. We are, perhaps, too unaware of the imaginative impact of the primary act of worship, the Mass, when the priest faced away from the people and toward the altar. What this said, in a way that could be felt as well as heard, was that the divine presence was mediated. At the same time, by way of statues, pictures, and prayers, devotional exercises evoked those feelings whether sexual, fraternal, or filial, that are humanly associated with intimacy, and which, in the context of prayer, suggested intimacy with the divine. But it was, again, a mediated intimacy, for it was primarily intimacy with God's saints that was evoked.

In such a religious context, to be a friend of God was not an item of much import. When the major avenues of access to God are in fear and trembling, the mark of true belief is not friendship. Reverence and obedience are perhaps the greater virtues in such a context. Keeping in mind that for Catholicism with its sacramental bias, what is valued most centrally will be enacted sacramentally, nothing in sacramental practice suggested that intimacy with God was of primary value. One approached the table of the Lord fasting, and only after vigorous self-scrutiny. Neither the practice of the rite of the Mass nor the devotional prayers used by people while it was happening suggested that the people were being welcomed primarily as the intimate friends of God. Moreover, there was no expectation, either official or social, that those devotions most suggestive of intimacy with God were in any way normative for the style of lived faith. Reverence and obedience were the values most thoroughly inculcated in the patterns of prayer and ritual. One did not have to worry about how friendly one felt oneself to be with God.

Liturgical change brought with it the suggestion, if not the experience, that our relationship with God will be one of intimate friendship. The stance of the priest facing the people over the altar projects, ideally if not factually, a model of ministry that is one of familial sharing. Since ministry is always an icon of what our relationship is conceived to be, then the modeling of an intimate model of ministry inevitably presses us to the question of our relationship to God.

The inescapably personal character of the God of the Bible has also had its impact upon the Catholic imagination since Vatican II. Biblical text, not only in rite, but also in theology, and with equal significance, in catechetics, and in piety, has taken a place in Catholic life that it never had before Vatican II. The translation of the scriptures so as to be read aloud in church services is only the ritual counterpart to a new attention to the scriptures in Roman Catholicism. We not only hear more of the scriptures in church; we also study them more frequently and take them more seriously as texts for prayer and meditation. More and more, biblical texts are becoming part of ordinary Catholic piety. Living encounter with evangelical Protestantism, obviously but not exclusively through charismatic renewal, has given the Bible a new place in ordinary Catholic life.

And, as everybody who opens a Bible knows, God is relentlessly spoken of as a present God, as palpable as Pittsburgh and as active as an earthquake. It is virtually impossible *not* to speak of the God of the Bible in personal terms. And that God is a God who is not to be tamed by the polite channels of ritual and devotion or to wait for the ministration of the officially ordained. He meets His people with relentless immediacy.

How this is translated into a God who is primarily lover, friend, companion, and parent is not difficult to understand, far as this may be from the intention of many biblical texts. In our own culture, the meaningfully personal is almost always the intimately personal. Moreover, the religious culture which has had the strongest influence on popular hearing and viewing of the scripture is that of evangelical Protestantism, whose gentle Jesus often blocks out perception of the ferocity of many of the biblical portrayals of God. Bring these cultural factors into conjunction with the sentimental residue of the place in Catholicism where a sense of intimacy flourished — popular devotions — and the results is a reading of the biblical personalism as if it spoke mostly of a God who is friend, lover, companion, and parent.

In view of the present situation, to say nothing of the spiritual tradition we have inherited since Bernard of Clairvaux, who in many ways invented "evangelical" piety, there is no point to advocating that we do away with language which suggests that God is a person whom we intimately know. There is a truth to that sort of language, and the inherited wisdom suggests that in many ways it is a better way to articulate what we know of God and ourselves than any other way. In any case, my own point is not to plead for the abolition of "personalist" spiritual language, but simply to make room for those for whom it is a problem.

How then can room be made for people who are uncomfortable about speaking of God as friend, lover, companion, parent, especially in articulating their own spiritual journey, or in how they care to approach private prayer? Are they religious deviants, or may we speak of a genuine "agnostic" spirituality as an appropriate spirituality for some Christians, perhaps many? In the first place, it needs to be said, more often than it is, both from the pulpit and in the study, as in the classroom, that all of our language about God limps, that in technical terms it is analogous language. To say or imply that God is our friend is not to suggest that we are somehow going to feel a divine arm over our shoulder. Such language is simply the best image we can find for a reality and an experience beyond the limits of human speaking.

Often enough, what is at work in the refusal to accept a speaking of God as friend and agent in one's life is an unnamed spiritual concern to preserve the sense of mystery. What is often seen too readily as a refusal of faith can in fact be the offering of a stance of reverence before mystery too profound to confine by words. For instance, I know somebody whose life was radically changed after a serious auto accident, which he survived through an unusual course of events. He is deeply aware of the import of the event in his life, yet finds himself uneasy when people say "God rescued you." The simple "God rescued you" is experienced as too glib, a language too *small* for the event. Among other things, it readily makes God arbitrary and capricious when one jumps too readily to such affirmations. For if God rescued this young man, why didn't he rescue countless thousands of others who died in auto accidents that year? The quiet respect for the event as mysterious and important is perhaps a more adequate response religiously and spiritually than a literalistic interpretation of it could ever be.

It also must be acknowledged that the ability to feel that God is present as friend, lover, companion, or parent, is essentially an imaginative ability that has nothing necessarily to do with the reality of things. Given the appropriate direction of my imagination, I can be brought to feel that Hitler is in my dining room or that leprechauns are dancing on my bedpost, but the ability to imagine such things as so, and to feel them, has nothing to do with their reality. To be able to feel that God is present as friend, lover, companion, or parent, only speaks for a certain power of the imagination, not for one's spiritual condition.

Even people who possess this power may be reluctant to use it. If they are reflectively aware that they are simply exercising their own imaginations, they may feel so foolish doing it that they may be incapable of taking such exercises seriously as moments of prayer. They will protest "I feel like I'm talking to myself." The conventional wisdom is to tell people that we always pray to God through the medium of images in one way or another, so that our own self-constructed image of his personality is perfectly acceptable as a vehicle of prayer. But surely this begs the question totally. The issue is not acceptability of less than adequate forms of prayer as far as God is concerned. One assumes that from his point of view, all our efforts are mere stammers. The issue is the acceptability of the pattern to the prayer. Surely there is nothing so absolute about private vocalization that it has in any way to be enjoined on all believers. People who cannot be comfortable with the conventional image of prayer as speaking to God should be encouraged to seek other modes of private prayer.

Part of the experience of this sort of spirituality is an intense intuition of there being something elusive, haunting, indirect, yet utterly compelling, and about which life relentlessly revolves. There is a sense of being drawn or pursued by something that is never quite tangible, that never quite allows any sense of a face to face meeting. It is more of a force, an elusive *something,* unnameable, and inscrutable, yet demanding the full attention of *my* person. There is a strong sense of mission or vocation, often itself a burden because the sense of mission or vocation so far exceeds possibilities and resources. There is a constant sense of being fascinated by religious questions, while not experiencing oneself as particularly religious, and not finding many of the conventional forms and expressions of religion particularly appealing. Often enough, there is a deep desire for prayer, but conventional patterns are experienced as foolish, inauthentic. The world is experienced against a horizon of mystery, yet the naming of that mystery as "God" is felt as somehow saying too much and too little — too much because it would obliterate the value of things in themselves, in all their secular simplicity, and too little because it would be to speak of God too glibly. Anne Morrow Lindbergh's *A Gift from the Sea*, Lewis Thomas' *The Medusa and the Snail*, and Annie Dillard's *Pilgrim at Tinker Creek* and *Holy the Firm* speak eloquently for this sort of religious perception, as do the writings of Ernest Becker and Elie Wiesel.

For such a religious consciousness, the forms of ritual prayer are a saving grace. There is a certain comfortable "impersonality" about sharing in a rite. One can act piously without feeling so, and the gestures are of such modesty that this can be done without feeling inauthentic. The careful doing of the action, in cooperation with others, relieves the worshipper of the strain to cultivate an intimate style of prayer. But perhaps far more important, ritual prayer is also congruent with the kind of religious consciousness I have described. God is addressed as present person, yet through the medium of fixed texts and inherited rites. Thus rite articulates and focuses the ambiguity of the experience of divine presence/absence. The rite is both personal and impersonal at the same time. Likewise, the rootedness of ritual in concrete things — bread, wine, water, oil, artifacts and gestures — speaks to and for a world experienced as having a value in its own right yet existing against a horizon of mystery. And so this spirituality will be at home with gesture and formal text much more than with spontaneous prayer. This is perhaps the reason why many otherwise not-so-conservative young people will prefer an antique form of ritual. Many contemporary liturgies are gesturally impoverished.

Likewise, for people of this bent, private moments of prayer are better prized for their setting than for their content. A walk in the woods or by the shore may be more appropriate than any sort of formal or conventional mediation. Likewise, listening to music or the contemplation of pictures or the reading of poetry or literature (none of them necessarily "religious") or yoga exercises (not necessarily prayer postures) will often be much more conducive to the attunement of such people to the movement of God in their lives than more explicit and conventional patterns of prayer. Their vocation is to live before God as mystery, not as friend, or more accurately perhaps, they are called to befriend the mystery that haunts them. Conventional exercises of prayer are often distractions from this essential task.

Such people are often distressed by these prayer patterns, congenial as they may be to them. They feel that this is not enough, not sufficiently "Christian." What they deserve is reassurance that their patterns are indeed quite appropriate. To force them into any other mold is to work contrary to the real movement of the Spirit in their lives. One aspect of the biblical experience of God is precisely what they experience constantly — an elusiveness, an absence, a tantalizing carrot on a stick, something inscrutable, just out of reach. In the Old Testament, the desert, the place of emptiness, is the primary place of meeting with God, as the cloud, with its hint of darkness and obscurity, is one of the prime symbols of the divine presence. In the New Testament, the event which renders Christ accessible to us is his resurrection from the dead. Yet the New Testament accounts of that central event are fraught with a sense of his elusiveness, of his going away. The stories of the empty tomb do not suggest only the joy of his conquest of death, but also the loss, not only of his ordinary daily presence, but even of the relic of it in the tomb's no longer containing his body. The risen Lord is the One who goes before the disciples — into Galilee, and to the right hand of the Father. The suggestion is less of a beloved presence than of a driving absence or the calling forth of a longing in the disciples.

The language of piety and spirituality has so come to prize a sense of being personal friend, lover, and companion of Jesus that spiritually sensitive people readily feel downright impious and irreligious when they find that this sort of language does not speak to their own experience. Unconventional as a piety which cannot relate to Jesus as to a present person intimately known may seem to be, there is nothing inimical to the biblical witness in such a stance. In the New Testament, the primary unitive relationship of believers to Christ is *not* for the purpose of making them his friends, but to make them one with the Father. In terms of things that are within the power of the believer to do something about, the issue is not what is felt or imagined in prayer, but what sort of life-stance is adopted. What is most important and central in "experiencing Jesus" is not to feel that he is an intimate friend, but to live in the communion of the faithful, living out his message and by his values. Too often, it is forgotten that since the resurrection, the authentic experience of Jesus is in the power of his Spirit. What it means to experience that is best summed up in the following lines of Karl Rahner; he describes the real attestation of the work of the Spirit as occurring when:

> ... a single sustaining hope enables us to face courageously both the enthusiastic highs and the depressing lows of our earthly existence; when a responsibility freely accepted continues to be carried out, though it no longer bears any visible promise of success or usefulness; when a human being not only experiences but willingly accepts the last free choice of his death; when the moment of death is recognized as a fulfillment of the promise of life; when we no longer have any proof of the total value of our life's actions, and yet have the strength to view them as positive in God's eyes; when the fragmentary experiences of love, beauty and joy can quite simply be experienced as a continued promise of love, beauty and joy; when the bitter and disap-

pointing and trying events of every day are endured serenely and patiently even to the last day, sustained by a strength whose source is forever elusive...when one has reached the point of entrusting all his certainty and all his doubts to the silent and encompassing mystery that he now loves above his personal achievements... This is where we truly find God and his liberating grace, where we experience what we Christians call the Holy Spirit.[1]

To acknowledge God as Father is not to have any sort of intuition of a cosmic Santa Claus. It is, rather, to live by the wellspring of hope that is in us, trusting the signs of dawn in ourselves and in the world rather than those of night. Surely it is in this spirit that Jesus commended himself to his Father on the cross.

And in the New Testament language of prayer, a sense of loss, of absence and of longing, is as much in evidence as a sense of divine presence. St. Paul's description of the work of the Spirit in the eighth chapter of the epistle to the Romans, with its description of the Spirit crying out in us with eager longing hardly speaks for a sense of divine presence: it suggests, rather, a sense of brokenness and incompleteness. Moreover, for St. Paul, the prayer of Christians is summed up in the cry *Maranatha.* Whether it means "The Lord is coming" or "Come, Lord," it speaks for a Lord who is longed for, not possessed. Far from being inimical to New Testament faith, a sense of the divine absence and elusiveness is inherent, even central in it. Such, certainly, is the spirit of the Lord's Prayer. Its whole direction is toward owning a sense that the signs of the kingdom of God are fragmentary and incomplete. By petitioning for the coming kingdom, it speaks for an attitude which hopes in the face of the ambiguity of this world.

We can note, with Simone Weil, that the presence of God

[1]Karl Rahner, S.J., *A New Baptism in the Spirit: Confirmation Today.* (Denville, N.J.: Dimension Books, 1975), pp. 23-26.

and his Christ is signed in a premier way under the impersonal forms of bread and wine, as the earnest of the feast of the heavenly kingdom is but a taste of bread, a sip of wine.

Much of the tension which surrounds and invades eucharistic celebration reflects a failure to have grappled with the kind of sense of the presence of God which I have attempted to explore here. It is inherent in the contemporary experience of God that God will be experienced in a diffuse way, even in prayer. Often enough, the problem of ritual prayer, especially eucharistic prayer, is not the ritual itself, but the way we approach it, the kinds of attitudes that we bring to it.

For instance, in context of the contemporary experience of God, God will inevitably be "faceless," met by indirection. The use of a formal prayer text allows expression both of the need to pray and of the sense that God is not quite like that — not a person in the same sense that another human being is a person, not present as we are present to one another. We can use the formal text because it is both ours (we are saying it) and not ours (somebody else composed it) and that sort of experience is congruent with our experience of God as present but not present as an ordinary human experience. The same is true of biblical readings. If we would recognize them for what they are — not directly words of God to us, but translations of the word of God to other people, we could relax with the difficulties and tensions the text presents and enter into a real dialogue with the text. We could take the reading of the scriptures as an overhearing, and seek to find in our own hearts, not carbon copies of the biblical experience, but echoes welling from resonances with other experiences at other times.

We need to recognize, too, that the whole point of having real ministers speak the texts is that the text functions as a vehicle of the speaker's own witness of faith. The priest at prayer or the reader at proclamation is as much a part of the event as the text itself; they are bearing witness to their own faith — the text is simply (though not solely) the script for their witness. The insistence upon putting leaflet missals in people's hands tends to block prayer at this level. By riveting people's attention on the literal words, we remove them from dealing with the sticky concreteness of grappling with God's presence as it is radiated through these broken and incomplete ministers and people here and now.

Perhaps one of the greatest disservices of old prayer books was the incessant questioning about "distraction" in prayer, which gave most people the idea that the point of participation in worship was a closely riveted attention of the mind. This prizing of concentrated intellectual attention effectively blocks people from the kind of vulnerability to one another and to the event of worship that is essential if ritual prayer is to become genuinely communal prayer. For the point of communal prayer is not simply to attend to the text, but to the event itself. It is this which constitutes the full and active participation of mind and body promoted by Vatican II's Constitution on the Liturgy and the present Order of Mass.

EPILOGUE

As I have attempted to suggest, the current direction of both liturgical reform and of contemporary popular piety is not only desirable but necessary. It is true that there is still much to be done, both in the area of ritual (including speech and gesture, art and craft) and in the realistic building of viable forms of community for the future. These are not separate issues. Ritual is the language by which a believing community identifies itself, while it is only in the attention to building community that we have anything worth saying to one another as Christians.

In the passing of older forms of worship, we may well experience loss and longing. Certainly, the old liturgy which passed with Vatican II had a certain coherence and beauty which the new one lacks. Yet it is in the halting gestures and raw stammering speech of contemporary worship that we must find a new sense of Christ's real presence. We must learn to identify Christ's presence, not so much with the splendor of marble and gold, nor in the sonority of an antique tongue, as with the blessed yet broken coming together of God's people. It is precisely the *sense* of mystery that we have lost, not its reality. For we have failed to identify and name that darker and more elusive presence of Christ among us. To continue to fail to do so is to court idolatry. For idolatry is not the worship of God under the veils of images and sacraments. Idolatry is the attempt to confine the divine presence to one image or one particular manifestation.

I have attempted to suggest, too, that our whole tradition has come to a critical turning point that will leave us liturgically uncomfortable for a long time to come — and should.

The old liturgy's prevailing image of a God who comes to us from outside with manipulative power has become morally repugnant as well as emotionally untenable. The Holocaust of a generation past is the cross of fire which must illumine, however painfully, a contemporary understanding of God. After that event, the human perception of evil in the world cannot be the same as it was before, as religious perception must irrevocably undergo change. A god who could, but did not, save his people is a god who, if he existed at all, would be unworthy of worship. What father, Jesus asked once, would give his son a stone if he asked for bread, or a scorpion if he asked for an egg? What god, we must ask, would command active caring for others as the heart of the worship of him, and yet "permit" the destruction of innocents. While this may be reconcilable in terms of abstract metaphysics, it is not reconcilable in the experience of the human heart. That sort of behavior in a human parent would not even be defensible in a court of law; much less is it acceptable to Christian moral sensibility.

Once more, then, we are called away from the god of the philosophers and away from the god of our childhood imagination, and called to the worship of the God of Jesus Christ — the God who is to be found beyond the gates of death, the death even of our religiosity and pious imaginings, the God who is revealed more in the flickering constancy of the human heart than in the glory of the skies.

In the face of our situation, the old metaphors of sacrifice and atonement crack badly. It is doubtful that sacrificial language has any immediate significance for a technological world, as a language of atonement becomes difficult before the silence of God. Yet it is precisely a God who haunts the very world we inhabit, whose elusive presence is found in the world of love and work and struggle and death, who is worth seeking in the strength of bread and the fleeting joy of wine, in the robustness of body and the tragedy of blood. The issue is not one of abandoning our basic liturgical language and gestures, but of learning the patience to be still enough to let them speak anew.

An inevitable sense of loss and longing may well attend our eucharistic prayer. We live thrown between the times. The faith of our ancestors will take a new shape in the lives of our children, and we have neither the security of a past achieved nor the assurance of a future in possession. The markings are few, many are the byways, and the kindly light is a flickering one.

Yet this is what it is to celebrate the resurrection. The risen Lord is not to be found among the dead relics of the past, and he goes before us to the place of his own people's future. People who are serious about the future of the church and its liturgy often ask themselves if they are simply moving deck chairs around on a slowly sinking Titanic. The appropriate answer may be "perhaps." But the engineers on the Titanic stayed in the engine room to keep the lights going as long as possible for the survivors. They were still burning and still illumined the night when the Titanic had sunk beneath the waves. The only present lampstand for the light of the world is the church we have and the liturgy we have received. They may well be enough. New wine, Jesus once observed, can only burst old skins. The saying has frequently been abused and interpreted as a warning. But on the lips of Jesus, it was fraught with promise. And the new wine of the Spirit gives every sign of flowing out of the cracked and crusted chalice of the church's past.